31/8/95

All-Colour

Food Combining Recipes

All-Colour

Food Combining Recipes

Healthy and slim with Dr. Hay

New recipes by Ursula Summ

foulsham

Contents

Foreword 5

Food Combining — Nutrition of the Future 6
   Experience of food combining 6
   What is decisive in food combining? 6
   The principle of separation 8

Harmonious and Wholefood Diet 9
   Wholefood: what does it contain? 9
   The first steps in wholefood 10
   Is meat really an energy provider? 10
   What is meant by over-acidity 11

Food Combining in Practice 12
   A Day of Purifying 12
   Food combining plan 14
   Quantity plan 16
   A day of combining 18
   Combining foods in a restaurant, on a
     journey and in canteens 19
   Shoots and sprouts, grow-your-own 20
   Shoots and sprouts as vitamin providers 21
   Tips on the recipes 21

Notes on the Recipes 23

Breakfast Ideas, Snacks and Desserts 24

Starters, Salads and Soups 46

Carbohydrate-rich Main Meals 64

Protein-rich Main Meals 100

Index 126

Foreword

Do you know the exhilarating feeling of well-being that makes you think you have wings? This is the message I am hoping to put across to you in this book, and I hope to prove how easy it can be to feel well and happy, mentally and physically, emotionally and psychologically.

There is no need to have a guilty conscience when you tuck into a hearty meal; when you *don't* want to go on a strict calorie-counted diet; when you have a drink or two for pleasure and relaxation; when you turn your back on a rigorous daily routine of physical exercise. I, too, like to eat chocolate or ice-cream occasionally, find morning exercise boring and hate dong anything which is unsuited to my temperament. It's natural!

From my personal experience, I know now that the secret of health and happiness lies in the simple things of everyday life. Many seek this in modern medicine without recognising that the solution to a good number of problems lies in a change of lifestyle. If you take this route and look for acceptable compromises, you will rid yourself of bad habits and take on better ones.

Do not try to change your eating style and pattern instantly, but gradually introduce healthy foods into your diet. Act patiently and thoughtfully and never in haste, otherwise all your good intentions and resolutions will fall by the wayside. Think positively and optimistically and good health will follow automatically.

Learn to appreciate yourself and be kind to your body. Develop your own personality, little by little gradually building up a mosaic of harmony.

No one asks us to suffer. We should try much harder to be happy and content, as only in this way can we radiate peace and serenity and influence others positively.

Laughing changes people far more than any other expression of emotion. And not just outwardly, but also inwardly. Hearty laughter encourages the blood to circulate, and this in turn helps to keep organs and the immune system in trim. It is also true to say that laughter is infectious and one of the simplest ways of spreading a little happiness all round.

Try to avoid moodiness. For example, do not let jealousy or feelings of hate control your thoughts and infect your soul. A bad thought attracts others, and before you know it you may be subject to emotional disturbance. Such distress often lasts for a long time and has more severe effects than a physical illness.

Trust your strength of will and believe in the healing power of positive thinking. Within each person there is far more than appears superfically. The ability to grow out of oneself is, in reality, a potential that lies dormant in each and every one and is there for the asking when we need help and guidance.

Discover for yourself the pleasant effect of correct breathing, beautifully scented aromas, harmonious colours and gentle contact with loved ones. Discover thankfulness again.

I would like to conclude my foreword by telling you briefy about myself and my experiences. In 1980, I discovered food combining and tried it out. Considerably over weight and bothered by troublesome metabolic conditions and disorders, It put me on the right road to a healthy life. I had, or so it appears to me today, stumbled upon a wonderful secret. For ten years I passed on everything I knew about harmonious eating habits and all the benefits I had experienced. As a result of conversations with specialist and participants in my groups, I learned much, and now I offer my especial thanks to all my friends and colleagues for all their willing co-operation and help.

Food Combining — Nutrition of the Future

Cooked meats belong to protein-rich foods.

Most types of vegetable belong to the neutral food group.

Cereals and cereal products are carbohydrate foods.

Experience of Food Combining

As a result of observations I have made since 1981, I have come to the conclusion that the way we combine foods in our diet is the only way ahead for healthy eating. More and more people are attempting to change their eating patterns to improve their health and now accept that a diet based on natural foods keeps the body physically and psychologically fit.

We have to thank the American doctor, Howard Hay, for giving us his concept of a harmonious and healthy way of eating. During his thirties, he suffered from a serious kidney disease and the doctors were unable to help him. For a long time he tried to analyse his own disease. He examined the chemical combination of the human body and discovered that it consisted of up to 80 per cent alkaline and 20 per cent of acid elements. He thus arranged his everyday food in the same proportion, eating largely alkaline, rather than acid-producing foods, and separarated those foods with a high carbohydrate content from those rich in protein. The unbelievable happened: as a result of proper separation and combining of certain foods it was possible for him to treat his own severe illness.

For years I have been offering courses for the overweight and I can confirm the value of this way of eating from my own experience with members of my groups. Not only did those suffering from kidney diseases experience improved health by changing their eating habits, but also those with metabolic disorders, and those suffering from rheumatism, migrane, circulatory disorders, menopause problems, inner disquiet and eczema. The overweight lost weight sucessfully, raised cholesterol dropped, and many patients were able to stop taking medicines. However, it is, of course, essential to seek the approval of your own doctor before following the diet, and this applies especially to diabetics, and anyone else with an organic disease or disorder.

Knowing how sucessful food combining can be, many GPs and alternative practitioners have recommended my courses to their overweight and obese patients and, despite lack of scientific proof to date, many health farms, spas and beauty clinics offer this eating regime to their clients with encouraging results.

What Is Decisive Food Combining?

The main characteristic, as the name suggests, is combining the correct foods in the correct proportions. In simple terms, food that consists largely of protein must be kept separate from carbohydrate foods whenever possible. This prevents 'confusion' in the digestive system and ensures a comfortable and stress-free passage of the food taken in. As a result, constipation and indigestion are lessened and excess body weight is lost without following strict slimming diets or buying costly ingredients. Growing children, especially those with sensitive stomachs, also benefit from food combining as opposed to 'mixed up' meals.

Let us look a little more closely at the digestive processes. With the help of digestive juices and enzymes produced by a number of organs, the food we eat is broken down to its smallest constituents which can, for example, be transported from the intestines to the liver. The body then reconstructs these to suit its own designs and needs, or breaks them down in order to provide energy.

If we follow, in stages, the way food passes through our body, we shall then understand what mistakes can lead to by disturbing the harmony of our bodies.

The first stage takes place in the mouth. This is where the pre-digestion of starch, a complex carbohydrate, begins. If, for instance, one chews a piece of bread for a long time, a sweet taste will become evident. This is due to the reaction of salivary amylose or ptyalin, a salivary enzyme, which works in an alkaline environment and breaks down the carbohydrate into smaller parts called maltose. Starch is found in large amounts in cereals, bread, potatoes, pasta, rice and pulses. In order to assist the pre-digestion of carbohydrates, food should be chewed long and slowly.

The second digestive process takes place in the stomach. This is where the protein foods such as meat, poultry, eggs, dairy products and fish are first pre-digested with the help of hydrochloric acid and the enzyme pepsin, and are broken down into smaller constituents.

According to Dr Hay, the digestive processes are disrupted when carbohydrates are consumed in concentrated form at the same time because the effectiveness of the digestive enzymes is reduced. The mechanical and chemical stimulation of food reaching the stomach starts off the production of hydrochloric acid and pepsin in the stomach.

If we only eat carbohydrates, just a small amount of acid juices are produced in the stomach. This allows the amylose to work more effectively, making carbohydrate foods easier to digest. It is worth noting at this stage that the results of badly combined foods can be heartburn, a feeling of fullness, flatulence and indigestion.

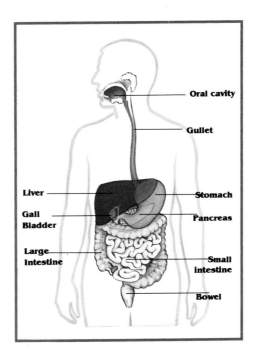

The human digestive system.

The next and third stage is when the food passes into the duodenum from the upper part of the intestine. It is here that the pancreas swings into action, its enzymes working alongside additional enzymes from the gall bladder and liver to further aid digestion. The work of pancreas is roughly divided into two parts. The hormone insulin and the hormone glucagon are produced and then released into the blood as required to regulate the blood sugar level. Secondly digestive enzymes are formed: trypsin which breaks down protein, pancreatic-amylose which breaks down carbohydrates, and lipase which breaks down fats. Afterwards, the mix is released into the small intestine. So that the complicated and varied digestive processes function efficiently, it is wise not to over-indulge in rich foods.

The mucous membrane inside the small intestine is covered with millions of villi, tiny hairs which take on board the digested material which pass them into the blood and the lymph systems.

The liver is comparable to a chemical factory. It processes all incoming materials, including some which the body does not need, such as alcohol.

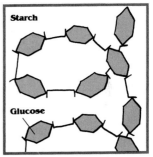

In common with other major nutrients, starch is broken down by enzymes and the end product is glucose.

Unfortunately it cannot send anything back, so foods which are unfavourably combined not only over-burden the digestive system, but also tax important organs of the body such as the liver.

The Principle of Separation

Food combining means harmonising one food with another and ensuring that the whole process of digestion takes place in an orderly fashion. Separation is not an overly complex task, and on pages 14 and 15 you will find a detailed plan showing proteins in blue and carbohydrates in red. Neutral foods are shown in grey. The neutrals can partner protein as well as carbohydrate foods and they include dairy produce, poultry, meat and fish. For health reasons all the above should be eaten sparingly, although the ultimate decision rests with you.

Neutral foods, for the purpose of food combining, are ones that do not interfere with the digestion of either carbohydrates or protein. They harmonise with all foods. There are what might appear to be discrepancies and contradictions in this statement, but rest assured that all aspects have been tried and tested over a long period of time and are based on personal experience. For instance, milk is a protein food, but when it turns sour, the action of souring turns it neutral; and likewise other foods, so you must be prepared to accept the charts. Fat and oils are digested not in the stomach but in the upper part of the small intestine and therefore are rarely responsible for indigestion or discomfort. The same applies for rich and fatty foods which should only be eaten in limited amounts as they are fattening and not vital constituents of a well balanced and pleasing meal.

Dr Ludwig Walb, the most significant representative of Dr Hay's diet in Germany, called this 'food separation'. This has lead to a number of misunderstandings worldwide, as a 100 per cent separation of protein and carbohydrates is neither possible, nor is it attempted in this diet. The term 'harmonious eating' would probably have been much more fitting, as it is the proper and harmonious combination of foods that leads to good digestion and that is the main aim of the Hay eating plan.

Citrus fruits belong to proteins.

Butter and cream are neutral.

Potatoes are carbohydrate-rich, so are cereals.

Harmonious and Wholefood Diet

Wholefood: What Does It Contain?

It has been known for some time now that heavily processed foods such as white flour, white sugar and polished rice only contain small amounts of valuable nutrients, as vitamins, minerals and fibre fall victim to the effect of food processing. For this reason wholefood is recommended; this means that one eats natural foods whenever possible, often raw or lightly and delicately cooked. The major part of any diet should consist of vegetable foods, such as salads, vegetables, potatoes, fruit, wholewheat cereals and products made from them, brown rice and cold-pressed oils such as extra virgin olive oil. With a diet that is largely based on these foods, and with milk products, meat and meat products acting as accompaniments, we provide our bodies with adequate amounts of vitamins, minerals, enzymes and fibre: life's essentials.

Here I must pause briefly and pass on one important observation. From my experience over many years, I know that there are very many people who are unable to take a strictly wholefood diet. For example, anyone with a damaged intestine can change their diet only very slowly as the higher fibre content of wholefood diets can pose special difficulties and lead to flatulence. Anyone with a sensitive stomach should first experiment with raw vegetables, and assess which suits them best. Any foods composed of fresh cereals should also be eaten with care. At the outset, food should be limited to salads and lightly cooked vegetables. Additionally, anyone suffering from an enzyme deficiency should take great care when switching to a wholefood diet. Every piece of food should be chewed carefully and new foods only eaten in small quantities. With care sensible food combining can benefit, but you must take account of your own particular circumstances.

Eat plenty of vegetables, raw or lightly cooked.

Salads are ideal as raw food.

The First Steps in Wholefood

If you are a beginner to wholefood I recommend that you tackle the diet plan slowly and cautiously, following it through one step at a time.

To start with, choose easily digestible cereals such as wholewheat. Have you ever baked or cooked using wholemeal flour? It is well worth trying. I like working with wholewheat products and have included it in some of the recipes in the book, both sweet and savoury. The fine, nut-like taste of wholemeal flour is pleasantly acceptable to almost everybody. Wholemeal flour should be used up quickly to prevent loss of flavour and vitamins. It should also be stored in an airtight container. For your first attempt at baking with wholemeal flour, choose a light biscuit with the addition of ground almonds or ground hazelnuts. Baked goods based on wholemeal flour usually require more baking powder and yeast than those made with white flour, so always follow the recipe most carefully and do not take liberties with the quantities until you are familiar with the properties of the ingredients.

Wholewheat grain can be used in many different ways. When using it for the first time, soak 100g/4oz of the grain overnight in water. Simmer the next day for about 25 minutes in a little water.

Wholewheat grains.

Finally, remove the saucepan from the heat and leave the grains to swell for 30 minutes. This cooked wheat can be used as an addition to a spicy vegetable soup or as a snack between meals with thick soured cream and honey. Depending on taste a small sliced banana can also be added.

You will discover that wholefoods satisfy for a long time and offer more by way of flavour than ready-made or preserved foods. Healthy food does not mean going without good things but simply replacing them with something better.

Is Meat Really an Energy Provider?

A further important theme is the consumption of meat, sausages and other meat products. Meat, consumed in large quantities, is unhealthy. Recent research has led to the view that a high intake can lead to the build up of harmful deposits, in the body as meat, and especially meat sausages, are high in fat and calories as well as being high in cholesterol. Those who have a tendency towards gout can aggravate the condition by eating too much flesh food and this also applies to those who suffer from rheumatic conditions.

What Is Meant By Over-acidity?

According to Dr Hay, protein-producing foods such as meat, sausages, fish, eggs and cheese can produce unwelcome acids in the body; uric and carbonic are just two examples. It is preferable to tip the scales in favour of alkaline foods – vegetables, salads, fruit and sprouts – using proteins as an accompaniment, rather than the other way round. Also acid-producing are psychological pressures, stress, noise, fear and excessive sport, all factors one tends to overlook.

A healthy body is in a position to break down and rid itself of harmful substances from the liver and to expel them through the kidneys, lungs and skin. However, even the most fit person cannot sustain acid residues over a long period without ill-effects.

Now I would like to show you that with the recipes in this book, healthy eating can be a pleasure. Vegetables, various lettuces, sprouts and fruit offer a varied mosaic of meal combinations in which, occasionally, meat and fish are introduced as accompaniments. The alkaline-producing foods are those rich in vitamins, minerals and fibre and are, according to Dr Hay, able to neutralise surplus acids in the body. If we provide our body with all that is necessery for life and do not unduly overload it, this is the best prerequisite for keeping it healthy. On the other hand, a lack of essential nutrients can lead to tiredness, lethargy and depression.

Food Combining in Practice

Decide for yourself which diet you choose for purifying.

A Day of Purifying

Before you change your eating habits to follow the food combining system, I recommend one day's purification of the whole system.

As a direct result of the stimulus given to the metabolism through a change of diet, drawing pains in the joints and muscles may come about. This is the reaction of the body as it expels toxins. The aches should be short-lived but if they persist you should see your doctor.

For your day of purifying, you can choose between: a vegetable-lettuce cure, a potato juice cure, and a potato and vegetable soup.

Vegetable-lettuce Cure

Eat any lettuce and vegetables in season, raw or lightly cooked. Prepare everything without fat or salt, and season to taste with vegetarian stock powder. The amount of vegetables or lettuce you eat depends entirely on appetite.

Fruit Cure

Eat any fresh fruit except bananas until three o'clock in the afternoon in whatever quantity you need to satisfy your appetite. From five o'clock onwards eat two medium-sized bananas or two medium-sized potatoes cooked in their skins.

Potato Drink Cure

This form of purifying is the one I recommend above all to those who have a sensitive stomach.

Cook 450 g/1 lb of washed potatoes in about 2 1/3½ pts water (without salt). In the case of new potatoes, the thin skins can be eaten along with the potatoes; older potatoes should be peeled. Purée the potatoes with the cooking water and drink this throughout the day.

Potato and Vegetable Soup

This soup is made from 3 potatoes, 3 onions, 3 leeks, 1 piece of celeriac and 2 to 3 carrots. The exact weight of the ingredients does not matter.

Clean the vegetables the chop them. Place them in a saucepan and cover with water. Add fresh or dried herbs and spices to taste (caraway, garlic, parsley, marjoram, lovage), but no salt. Simmer, covered until the vegetables are soft. The soup can be seasoned to taste with some vegetarian stock powder. Eat as desired during the day.

Drinks

During this day of purifying you should drink plenty of fluids in the form of herbal teas – fruit tea, nettle tea or others – or mineral water (non-carbonated). With all the suggestions except the fruit, you may have a light breakfast.

Food Combining Plan

Within one meal, protein-rich **and carbohydrate-rich foods should** *not* **be mixed.**

Cooked mussels and shellfish are protein-rich.

Chanterelle and other mushrooms are neutral.

Protein

All types of cooked meat.
This includes:
Beef: All cuts.
Veal: Fillet, leg and breast.
Lamb and mutton: All cuts.
Pork is not recommended.
All cooked poultry.
This includes: rolled turkey roast, slices, breast, minced turkey, goose, duck, grilled chicken, chicken breast.
All wholemeat, continental sausages, sausages, corned beef and boiled ham.
Avoid any sausages made from pork.
All unsmoked types of fish, shellfish and cooked crustacean.
This includes: plaice, cod, haddock, salmon, tuna, mackeral, halibut, sole, herring, pike, trout, mussels, prawns, lobsters, crab.
All soy products.
This includes: tofu and any sandwich spreads but not soy sauce.
Eggs and milk.
All types of cheese up to 50 per cent fat.
This includes: Parmesan, Emmental, Edam, Gouda, Cheddar, Brie.
Cooked or canned tomatoes.
Drinks.
This includes: fruit tea, cider, dry white wine and Champagne.
All berry fruits (except bilberries).
All pipped fruits (except soft apples).
All stone fruit and citrus fruit.
All exotic fruits.
This includes: mangoes, kiwis, melons. These should be eaten by themselves, or combined, in small amounts, with protein foods. They make an excellent snack with milk or yoghurt
Tip
For coating food, use ground nuts or sesame seeds in preference to breadcrumbs.

Neutral Foods

Neutral foods can be mixed in a meal with protein-rich or carbohydrate-rich foods.

All fats.
This includes: oil (cold-pressed for preference), soft margarines with a high content of polyunsaturated fats, butter and fat-like vegetable spreads.
All soured milk products.
This includes: quark, yoghurt, thick soured full-cream milk, soured and sweet cream, buttermilk and fermented whey concentrate.
All types of cheese with at least 60 per cent fat.
This includes: fresh cheese made with double cream, other cream cheeses, Camembert.
All white types of cheese.
This includes: sheep's and goat's cheese, Mozzarella, cottage cheese.
All uncooked smoked sausage products.
This includes: non-pork salamis, frying sausages without pork, air-dried ham such as Parma, blood sausage (black pudding).
Uncooked meat.
This includes: beef tartare etc.
Uncooked marinated or smoked fish.
This includes: smoked herring, eel, mackerel, trout, smoked salmon and salted herring. Note that many products are high in salt.
Certain vegetables, salads and mushrooms.
This includes: aubergine, leaf artichokes, broccoli, cauliflower, green beans, green peas, fennel, cucumber, garlic, kohlrabi, leek, sweetcorn, carrots, peppers, radish, horseradish, beetroot, brussel sprouts, red cabbage, sauerkraut, celery, asparagus, spinach, raw tomatoes, white cabbage, savoy cabbage, onions,

courgettes, all types of lettuce (including iceberg lettuce, endive, chicory, Chinese leaves), oyster mushrooms, ordinary mushrooms, chanterelles, boletus and any other kind of mushroom.
All sprouts and shoots.
All fresh and dried herbs as well as all spices.
All nuts and seeds (except ground nuts).
This includes: hazel nuts, coconut flakes, almonds, pine nuts, sesame seeds and walnuts.
Bilberries, untreated raisins.
Olives.
Egg yolk.
Spirits.
This includes: gin, whiskey, brandy, white rum etc.
All gelatinous products.
This includes: gelatine, agar-agar, (sea algae; the powder is dissolved in a cold liquid, is heated to 60-80°c and left to cool), vegetable binder made of carob seed flour (from health shops).
Tips
Sauces for salads that are to be eaten with a protein meal, should be made from oil, cream, herbs and lemon juice. Sauces for salads that are to be eaten with a carbohydrate meal should be made from soured milk products such as thick soured full-creamed milk and yoghurt.

Carbohydrates

All cereals.
This includes: wholewheat, rye, barley, oats, unripe corn millet, sweetcorn and natural rice.
Buck wheat.
All wholewheat cereal products.
This includes: wholmeal bread and bread rolls, cakes of wholemeal flour, wholemeal pasta, wholemeal semolina.
Certain vegetables and fruit.
This includes: potatoes, Jerusalem artichokes, kale, salsify, bananas, untreated dried fruit (except for raisins-they are neutral), currants, fresh dates and figs, soft apples.
The following sweeteners.
This includes: frutrose, honey, maple syrup, pear and thick apple juice.

Miscellaneous items
This includes: potato starch, cream of tartar, custard powder, carob powder and beer.
Tip
Fried cereal cakes should be coated only in breadcrumbs, chopped nuts or sesame seeds and not be first coated with egg.

Foods to avoid
White flour and products made from it such as sweet and savoury confectionery as well as pasta.
Polished rice.
Sugar, sweeteners and products made from them such as sweets and jams; ready-made meals and preserves.
Dried pulses such as peas, lentils, beans.
Ground nuts and cranberries.
Pork and products made from pork.
Uncooked meat and raw egg white and products made from them such as ready-made mayonnaise.
Hardened fats such as normal types of margarine and firm white cooking fat.
Tea, coffee and cocoa.

Dr Hay discourages anyone with kidney diseases from eating large quantities of spinach, rhubarb, chestnuts, horseradish, mustard and pepper.

In general only eat small quantities of meat. This applies, too, to anything smoked or pickled as they contain substances which can promote the development of cancer. Whether you stop eating these things altogether is up to you.

Watch your intake of salt carefully. Too much salt is unhealthy, so go easy on sausages, cheese, ready-made products and some shop-bought bread.

Explanation of colours:

blue = protein meals, or protein-rich foods.
red = carbohydrate meals, or carbohydrate-rich foods.
grey = neutral meals or neutral foods.

Untreated dried fruit is carbohydrate-rich.

Avoid refined products such as sugar and white flour.

Quantity Plan

The weights and times in the plan are only an approximate guide and should be tried out by you.

Hunger and fasting are often meaningless and no-one should leave the table hungry as this is bound to result in snacking between meals.

Always remember: to remain healthy you need plenty of cooked and/or raw vegetables and salad as your overall healthy diet.

Eat muesli for a change in the morning.

A glass (about 200 ml/7 fl oz) of still mineral water.

Breakfast

There is a choice between a carbohydrate or protein meal or fruit.

Carbohydrate meal:
    1 slice wholemeal bread (50 g/2oz)
or 1 wholemeal roll
or 3 slices wholemeal crispbread
    spread thinly with butter
plus:
    25 g/1 oz sliced meat sausage
or 25 g/1 oz cheese
or 50 g quark
or 10 ml/2 tsp honey
or muesli (see page 29)

Protein meal:
2 eggs (fried, scrambled, boiled or poached)
(more than 4 eggs per week is not recommended)
plus tomatoes, cucumber, pepper, radishes or some other neutral vegetable but *no* bread

Fruit breakfast:
Fruit of the season (except bananas), eating as much as you like.

Anyone not wishing to give up tea or coffee should drink it with some cream or full cream milk. Honey should be used as a sweetener, if liked.
Important: Chew everything very well with plenty of saliva. Coffee or tea is no substitute for saliva.

A large cup of tea or a glass of still mineral water

A large cup of tea or a glass of still mineral water

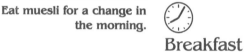

Between Meals

200 g/7 oz fruit in season (but no bananas)
or 300 ml/½ pint fresh milk or soured milk products
or 100 g/4 oz fruit and with 150 ml/¼ pint milk or soured milk product

A large cup of tea or a glass of still mineral water.

Midday Meal

For a midday meal you have a choice of a protein or a carbohydrate meal.

Protein meal:
    100-150 g/4-5 oz meat
or 150-200 g/5-7 oz fish
or 2 eggs
or 60 g/2½ oz cheese
or 75g/3 oz cooked meat sausage
plus 400 g/14 oz vegetables or salad based on lettuce.

Carbohydrate meal
    50 g/2 oz cereal
or 50 g/2 oz brown rice (uncooked weight)
or 50 g/2 oz wholemeal pasta (uncooked weight)
or 200 g/7 oz potatoes
plus 400 g/14 oz vegetables or salad based on lettuce

Can also be eaten with25-30 g/1-2 oz of neutral food (see the Food Combining Plan on pages 14-15 or the recipe section).

In addition to the ingredients of the protein or carbohydrate meal you can add small amounts of butter, margarine, oil or cream. They are neutral and perfectly suitable.

Do not drink when eating a main meal. Should you find this uncomfortable, drink a small glass of water in sips.

A large cup of tea or glass of still mineral water.

A large cup of tea or glass of still mineral water.

A large cup of tea or glass of still mineral water

Between Meals

    1 banana
or 1 sugar-free museli bar
or 1 piece cake (see pp. 32-34)
or 2-3 biscuits (see pp. 34-39)
or 1 slice crispbread with honey
or 20 ml/4 tsp quark with 5 ml/1 tsp honey
or 10 ml/2 tsp wholemeal oat flakes and 1 plain yoghurt
or 200 g soured milk products
Do not drink fresh milk products after 4.30.

A large cup of tea or glass of still mineral water.

Evening meal

In the evening you have a choice of carbohydrates:
    50 g/2 oz cereal
or 100 g/4 oz wholemeal bread
or 50 g/2 oz natural rice (uncooked weight)
or 50 g/2 oz wholemeal pasta (uncooked weight)
or 200 g/7 oz potatoes
plus 400 g/14 oz vegetables and lettuce, and 25-50/1-2 oz neutral foods and small quantities of butter, oil or cream.

Examples of carbohydrate meals are Mushrooms au Gratin (see page 86) and Mixed Vegetables on Rice (see page 86).
Home baked biscuits are suitable for eating between meals in the afternoon.

In the evening, eat a carbohydrate meal such as a Pizza Romana (see page 92).

A Day of Combining

Suggestions for Breakfast

Fruit in season (except bananas), as much as you like or a Muesli Crunch (see page 29)
or a slice of wholemeal bread, spread with butter and topped with cheese or sausage without pork. Instead you could spread the bread with 20 ml/4 tsp honey or quark.

Suggestion for First Snack Between Meals

1 piece of fruit in season (except bananas)
or something neutral between meals. For example a plain yoghurt or 1 piece of fruit (see Food Combining Plan pages 14-15)
or a protein food (see pages 40-43).

Suggestion for Midday Meals

A protein rich meal (see pages 100-125), for example: Fillet of Salmon with Vegetables (see page 121)
or Scrambled Eggs with Vegetable Salad (see page 108)
or Chicken Salad and Lentil Sprouts (see page 112)
or Hungarian Goulash (see page 118)
or a carbohydrate-rich meal (see pages 64-99)
For example Corn Dumplings with Sauerkraut (see page 95)
or Herrings in Cream with Potatoes (see page 72)
or Vegetable and Mushroom Fry (see page 84)
or Spaghetti on Vegetables (see page 81).

Suggestions for Second Snack Between Meals

1 banana
or 1 sweet (soft) apple
or something neutral between meals, for example quark or yoghurt with bilberries
or one vegetable (see the Food Combining Plan pages 14-15)
or carbohydrate between meals, for example a piece of cake or some biscuits (see pages 32-38).

Suggestions for Evening Meal

In the evening, more digestible carbohydrate meals are preferable. You could for example eat:
Rice Salad (see page 89)
or Mixed Pizza Breads (see page 94)
or Pizza Romana (see page 92)
or Onion Flan (see page 93)
or Mushroom Risotto (see page 84)
or Jacket Potatoes with Quark (see page 71).

For all those who do not have a great deal of time, it is a good idea to prepare enough ingredients for two meals at the same time. For example cauliflower: cook twice the amount and in this way it will be possible to use half a carbohydrate meal, (for example Cauliflower with Herb Butter and Potatoes) and the rest for a protein meal the next day, (for example Cauliflower Salad with Turkey Slices).

In the recipe section you will find a series of dishes that can be prepared very quickly. For example:
Potato and Leek Soup (see page 66)
Courgette and Potato Soup (see page 66)
Carrot and Potato Stew (see page 68)
Mixed Vegetables Salad (see page 76)
Mixed Pizza Bread (see page 94)
Jacket Potatoes with Quark (see page 71)
Fried Potatoes with Brussel Sprouts (see page 72)
Mashed Potatoes with Sauerkraut and Fried Onions (see page 72)
Almond Pancakes (see page 99)

Start the day with a good breakfast.

A nibble between meals will prevent you becoming hungry.

Salmon Fillet with Vegetables (see page 121) is a good choice.

Spaghetti with Garlic Cream Sauce (see page 79)
Tomato Salad with Scrambled Eggs (see page 110)
Grilled Vegetables (see page 102)
Grilled Cauliflower (see page 104)
Turkey Cream Steaks with Beans (see page 110)
Spinach and Minced Meat Bake (see page 115)
Plaice Fillets with Cucumber Salad (see page 125)

Tomato Salad with Scrambled egg, and Turkey Cream Slices with Beans (see page 110) are quick to prepare.

Meals Properly Combined

As Dr Hay discovered, our body consists of 20 per cent acid and 80 per cent alkaline elements. The conclusion he drew was that the best thing to do was to see that our daily meals should be combined in the same proportions. Thus should then consist of 20 per cent acid-forming foods and 80 per cent alkaline forming foods. This means in practice that a protein meal should consist of one part meat or fish or eggs or cheese (example 1 part= 100 g/4 oz and of three to four parts of vegetables. The vegetables can be eaten cooked or uncooked.

Accordingly, a carbohydrate meal of one part potatoes, natural rice or other cereal or wholegrain pasta (example one part = 100 g/14 oz and of three to four parts vegetables. Here also the vegetables can be eaten cooked or uncooked.

Acid-rich fruit, such as berries, stone and seed fruit as well as citrus fruit should, for reasons of digestion, never be eaten with the carbohydrate foods (see the Food Combining Plan on pages 14-15). Although these fruits belong to proteins, it has been shown that they should be combined in small quantities only with other protein-rich foods. They are particuarly good enjoyed for breakfast, snacks between meals, or on a hot day as a complete midday meal.

It is recommended that after 3 o'clock in the afternoon you do not eat any more fruit, except for bananas, bilberries or dried fruit, as this could easily lead to fermentation in the intestines.

Apples play a particular role in food combining. Freshly harvested they contain a higher fruit acid content and for this reason belong to the protein foods. A stored, soft, sweet apple on the other hand, can be mixed into a meal along with cereals, wholegrain noodles, brown rice or potatoes, that is to say carbohydrate foods. Soft apples can be used to make apple cakes, also for apple purée to be eaten with rice or noodles, or can enrich a muesli when grated.

Apples play a special role in food combining.

Combining Foods in a Restaurant, on a Journey and in Canteens

If you find food combining fun, and this way of eating does you good, then you will find it very easy, when in a restaurant, to put food combining principles into practice. A menu usually consists of meat dishes, accompaniments and salads. It is up to you to decide on a protein or carbohydrate meal. If you would like to eat meat, fish or something with eggs, then choose a protein meal, and so the right combination follows easily. Instead of the usual potatoes, rice or noodles, choose a double portion of salad or vegetables, which are neutral foods. If instead you prefer a carbohydrate meal, then the choice in most restaurants is not going to be very sumptuous. Choose potatoes, rice, noodles or bread and eat, with it smoked trout, smoked salmon, sheep's cheese or a herring dish, all neutral foods. Eat it with a large salad and plenty of vegetables.

When eating on holiday, in hotels and canteens you should proceed in the same way. Also here meat dishes as well as accompaniments and salads will be available. Again choose a protein or carbohydrate meal.

Those at work who do not have the facility of a canteen to eat, or prefer not to eat there , should take with them salads made up of tomatoes, cucumbers, peppers, cauliflower, Chinese leaves, kohlrabi, radishes, white or red cabbage, sauerkraut, fennel and other types of vegetables. To make a protein meal, combine them according to taste with roast beef, cold roast, chicken meat, eggs, cheese or fish; or prepare a herb-quark dip to go with it. For a carbohydrate meal suitable foods would be potato salad, rice salad, noodle salad, fried cereal cakes and bread.

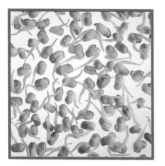

Mung bean sprouts.

Lentil sprouts.

Shoots and Sprouts – Grow Your Own

Type	Soaking time in hours	Number of rinsings per day	Sprouting time in days	Length of shoots	Approx. produce: seed
Adzuki beans	12	3	4	bean length	3:1
Alfalfa	8	2	7-10	max. 10 cm	5:1
Hartshorn clover	6-8	2	2	seed length	4:1
Buckwheat in husks	—	2	2-3	5 mm	3:1
Peas	12	2-3	3	pea length	2:1
Millet in husks	8	2-3	3	2 mm	1.5:1
Chick peas	12	3-4	3	5 cm	3-4:1
Cress	—	1	6-8	4 cm	2:1
Pumpkin	12	3	2-3	3 mm	2:1
Linseed	—	1	2-3	seed length	1.5:1
Lentils	8	2-3	3	2 cm	4-6:1
Mung beans	12	2-3	3-4	2 cm	5-6:1
Huskless barley	8	1-2	2-3	grain length	2:1
Huskless oats	4	2	2-3	grain length	2:1
Radish	—	2-3	3-4	3 mm	2-3:1
Rye	12	2	2-3	grain length	2:1
Mustard	—	1	2-3	up to 5 mm	2:1
Sesame	6	2	2	2 mm	1.5:1
Soy beans, yellow	12	3-4	3-4	bean length	4:1
Sunflower	6	2-3	2	grain length	2:1
Wheat	12	2	2-3	grain length	2:1

Shoots and Sprouts as Vitamin Providers

Shoots and sprouts are essentially small 'vitamin bombs'. While soaking and during the process of germination, enzymes in their grains which break down nutrients into their smallest constituents become active and, amongst other things, form vitamins. This provides the shoot with all the nutrients it needs for growth and repair – useful for us as well. Shoots and sprouts belong to neutral foods. They can be mixed into salads, sprinkled on to various sandwich fillings or mixed into muesli. Particulary in winter when many kinds of salad ingredients are grown under glass, the shoots are a valuable substitute. A variety of shoots and sprouts is now available in health shops and well-stocked supermarkets. However, it is easy to grow them yourself.

If you do not have special equipment for sprouting (there are a number of brochures available with instructions) you can use a preserving jar with excellent results.

This Is How It's Done

Suitable grains for sprouting (use the table on page 20 for this purpose) must be thoroughly washed and the dirt and broken grains removed. Pour plenty of water over the grains. Those that are infertile will float to the top and can then be scooped out and discarded. Place the grains in a preserving jar or glass, add plenty of water and cover with a muslin cloth. Fasten the cloth with a rubber band (see photographs). The grains must now be left to swell (in the case of buckwheat, cress, linseed, radish and mustard this is not necessary). How long is given in the table. After soaking, the water can be poured away (it is very good for watering flowers!) and the grains thoroughly rinsed. Finally, they should be shaken loose and the jar or glass placed diagonally with the opening downwards so that excess water can drain away. The seed is now left to sprout, the length of time depending on the type. They should be regulary rinsed (see table), it is important not to allow mildew to form.

Tips on Sprouting Seeds
- Sprouts should not be left in water, but be just damp.
- The grains should be left to sprout in a temperature of 18-22°c in a light place but out of direct sunlight. See the table for a guide as to how many days you need for harvesting.

Tips on The Recipes

- All the recipes that I have collected together in this book are easy to prepare. They are good examples of how protein-rich foods can be combined with neutral and carbohydrate foods.
- If you want to vary the recipes or put your own together, use the Food Combining Plan on pages 14-15 for guidance.
- You will find arrangement of food easy, as all the recipe titles are printed in different colours: the carbohydrate-rich meals in red, the protein-rich meals in blue and the neutrals in grey.
- All individual vegetables are taken to be medium-sized. When a weight is given, it is after peeling and trimming.
- The kilocalories (kcals) and kilojoules (kj) refer to one portion, in the case of confectionery, to one piece.
- The preparation time given in the recipes includes cooking time as well. It is only a rough guide as much depends on how quickly you work. When additional times for rising and soaking are required, these are given separately.
- A few of my recipes contain ingredients that may not be readily available in all supermarkets but which will be available in health food shops.

Leave seeds to soak if necessary.

Pour the water away after soaking.

Leave the surplus water to drain off well.

Season to suit your own taste.

Cold pressed natural oils are preferable.

- Vinegar is not recommended in food combining. Instead I use concentrated whey, lemon juice or lime juice.
- For binding and thickening, use arrowroot or cornflour.
- For salting I like to use sea salt. It contains minerals essential to life and trace elements such as iodine. Also herb salt is irreplacable as far as taste goes. It's cooking salt content is about 84 per cent
- Vegetarian vegetable stock powder is useful for sprinkling over dishes to give them more flavour – for example soups, sauces and vegetables.
- Smoked tofu, fried in hot sunflower oil, is delicious in almost all salads. It should be cut into dice before frying.
- In a few of my recipes you will find thick soured full milk. I have recently discovered that this product is unfortunately not available everywhere, so substitute yoghurt mixed with an equal amount of full cream milk.
- In combining foods, the choice and correct use of oils and fats play an important role. Natural products are recommended like cold-pressed unrefined oils. They contain valuable polyunsaturated fatty acids in large quantities. Olive oil, sunflower oil, wheat germ oil, linseed oil and maize oil all contain polyunsaturated fatty acids in good quantities. When cooking, use only olive oil and sunflower oil whenever possible as they can be heated with no problem. All the others should only be used cold, as for instance in salad dressings.
- Butter and unhardened vegetable fats (for example health food margarine with a high content of unsaturated fatty acids), are also recommended but should be used sparingly. They should never be overheated or strongly browned. Not recommended are all refined oils and hardened fats such as margarine and white cooking fat.

As everyone has different tastes, I want the seasonings in my recipes to be regarded as suggestions, season to suit your own taste. Now and again try out something new.

For those members of the family who do not want to join in food combining, it is not necessary to cook something extra especially for them. Add some fish or meat to your carbohydrate-rich meal or supplement the protein-rich meal with potatoes, rice or pasta. It is important as with any other form of diet to drink plenty. Take in 1 to 2 litres/1¾ to 3½ pints through the day in the form of mineral water or tea. From time to time you can drink a glass of wine or beer.

When food combining, you will have no 'performance break' after a meal. Even after a fairly rich meal you will feel fresh and fit. In the case of a mixed meal this can be quite different and fatigue may well ensue 20 to 30 minutes later.

Notes on the Recipes

1 Follow one set of measurements only, do not mix metric and Imperial.

2 Eggs are size 2.

3 Wash fresh produce before preparation.

4 Spoon measurements are level.

5 A tablespoon is 15 ml; a teaspoon is 5 ml.

6 Adjust seasoning and strongly flavoured ingredients, such as onions and garlic, to suit your own taste.

7 If you substitute dried for fresh herbs, use only half the amount specified.

Breakfast Ideas, Snacks and Desserts

In the following chapter you will find savoury breads and mueslis – for breakfast – as well as yoghurt and quark dishes, ice creams, mixed drinks, baked and other dishes which can be eaten between meals and as desserts. For further suggestions turn to pages 16 and 18.

Do not forget Dr Hays recommendation: acid-rich berries, citrus fruit, stoned fruit and cored fruit should not be eaten after 3 o'clock in the afternoon. If you do not want to eat fruit in the morning, or it does not agree with you, eat it in between meals or at midday. Combine it in small quantities with protein-rich food but never with carbohydrate meals. (see the Food Combining Plan on pages 14-15)

The old proverb is applicable to food combining: breakfast like an emperor, eat lunch like a king and dine like a beggar.

What is eaten in the morning and before lunch is used up by the body when it is at its most active. Anything eaten in the evening, or before any rest, can lead to increased weight, even if one has no particular problem in this direction.

Bread with Topping

Ingredients	Metric/Imperial
Soft butter	30 ml/2 tsp
Mature Camembert (60% fat)	150 g/5 oz
Onion, halved	1
Caraway seeds	5 ml/1 tsp
Paprika for sprinkling	
Wholemeal bread	4 slices

1. Beat the butter until creamy. Squash the Cambembert well with a fork and mix with the butter.
2. Chop half the onion very finely and cut the other half into thin slices.
3. Blend the chopped onion and the caraway seeds into the Camembert mixture. Arrange on a plate, garnish with the onion slices and sprinkle with paprika. eat with wholemeal bread.
(Photo top)

Preparation time: 10 mins
Serves 4
Approx. 240 kcal/1015 kJ

Tip
You can eat the bread with the topping along with a neutral fresh lettuce. It can also be served as a cold main meal for two people.

Quark Bread with Carrot Slices

Ingredients	Metric/Imperial
Quark (20% fat)	60 g/2½ oz
Mineral water	20 ml/4 tsp
Herb salt for seasoning	
Wholemeal bread	1 slice
Butter	5 ml/1 tsp
Carrot	1
Chopped fresh parsley	5 ml/1 tsp

1. Stir the quark with the mineral water until smooth and season to taste with herb salt. Spread the bread with the butter.
2. Peel the carrot and cut lengthwise into thin slices. Arrange the carrot slices on the bread, keeping one slice back for garnish, and top with the quark.
3. Cut the rest of the carrot into very thin sticks and sprinkle over the quark with the parsley.
(Photo bottom)

Preparation time: 10 mins
Serves 1
Approx. 230 kcal/955 kJ

Radish Bread

Ingredients Metric/Imperial

Wholemeal or rye bread	1 slice
Butter	5 ml/1 tsp
Radishes	6
Cottage cheese	75 g/3 oz
Chopped fresh chives	10 ml/2 tsp
Paprika for sprinkling	

1. Spread the bread with the butter. Cut the radishes into thin slices and arrange on top.
2. Spoon the cheese on top of the radishes then sprinkle with the chives and paprika.
(Photo top)

Preparation time: 10 mins
Serves 1
Approx. 150 kcal/635 kJ

Pick-you-up Roll

Ingredients Metric/Imperial

Wholemeal roll	1
Quark (20% fat)	75 g/3 oz
Mineral water	20 ml/4 tsp
Sea salt	
Butter	10 ml/2 tsp
Cucumber	8 thin slices
Bean sprouts (home made see page 21 or bought)	45 ml/3 tbsp
Paprika for sprinkling	

1. Cut the roll in half and toast.
2. Meanwhile stir the quark with the mineral water until smooth. Season with salt.
3. Spread the butter on to the toasted roll halves and top with cucumber slices. Arrange the quark on top and sprinkle with bean sprouts and paprika.
(Photo bottom)

Preparation time: 10 mins
Serves 1
Approx. 280 kcal/1180 kJ

Bread with Savoury Soft Cheese

Ingredients	Metric/Imperial
Wholemeal or rye bread	1 slice
Butter	5 ml/1 tsp
Lettuce leaves	2
Carrot	1
Hazel nuts	8
Soft cream cheese	50 g/2 oz

1. Spread the bread with butter and cover with the lettuce leaves.
2. Peel the carrot and cut into thin slices. Coarsely chop the hazelnuts and mix with the carrot.
3. Stir both into the cheese and spoon on to the lettuce leaves.
(Photo bottom)

Preparation time: 10 mins
Serves 1
Approx. 380 kcal/1585 kJ

Oat Flakes with Blueberries

Ingredients	Metric/Imperial
Rolled oats	50 g/2 oz
Thick Greek yoghurt	60 ml/4 tbsp
Fresh or frozen blueberries, thawed	150 g/5 oz
Clear honey	15 ml/1 tbsp
Cinnamon for sprinkling	

1. Tip the rolled oats into a bowl and mix with the yoghurt. Transfer to a dessert dish.

2. Combine the blueberries with the honey and a sprinkling of cinnamon.
3. Spoon on top of the oat and yoghurt mixture.
(Photo centre left)

Preparation time: 20 mins
Serves 1
Approx. 400 kcal/1665 kJ

Custard and Quark Pudding

Ingredients	Metric/Imperial
Whipping cream	150 ml/¼ pt
Water	350 ml/12 fl oz
Small packet of custard powder (without artificial colouring)	
Pinch of saffron	
Glucose syrup	45 ml/3 tbsp
Vanilla essence	5 ml/1 tsp
Quark (20% fat)	250 g/9 oz

1. Dilute the cream with the water. Mix the custard powder and the saffron in a cup then add the syrup. Gradually mix in 75 ml/ 5 tbsp of the cream mixture. Whisk gently to prevent lumps forming.
2. Heat up the remaining cream and water mixture until warm. Add the vanilla essence. Gradually whisk in the custard powder liquid. Bring to the boil, stirring all the time.
3. Mix in the quark little by little, pour into dishes and serve warm.
(Photo top)

Preparation time: 15 mins
Serves 4
Approx. 280 kcal/1180 kJ

Muesli Crunch

Ingredients	Metric/Imperial
Rolled oats flakes	250 g/9 oz
Blanched almonds	300 g/11 oz
Unpeeled sesame seeds	100 g/4 oz
Sunflower seeds	100 g/4 oz
Honey	250 g/9 oz
Cold pressed sunflower oil	10 ml/2 tsp
Warm water	100ml/3½floz
Raisins	250 g/9 oz

1. Tip rolled oats into a bowl.

2. Chop the almonds coarsely. Roast the sesame seeds in a frying pan without fat then leave to cool. Pre-heat oven to 160°C/350°F/gas mark 3.

3. Knead all the prepared ingredients together with the sunflower seeds, honey, oil and water.

Spread into a lightly oiled, shallow baking tray, making sure there are no thin patches.

4. Bake the muesli mixture for 1-1½ hours and stir every now and then to crumble up the mixture.

5. Leave to cool. Finally mix in the raisins and transfer to an airtight jar with well-fitting stopper. Muesli can be kept like this for several weeks. *(Photo centre right)*

Preparation time: 15 mins
Baking time: 1-1½ hrs
Makes about 26 × 50 g/ 2 oz portions
Approx. 195 kcal/815 kJ

Tip

This crispy muesli can be eaten for breakfast mixed with fromage frais, mild yoghurt or 10 ml/2 tsp cream and the same amount of water. To make a more filling breakfast, a banana can be added or a soft apple grated in. The crispy muesli can be eaten as above in between meals and is also good as a dry nibble.

Buttermilk Drink

Ingredients   Metric/Imperial

Small banana   1
Thick honey   10 ml/2 tsp
Cold buttermilk   300 ml/½ pt
Chopped   30 ml/2 tbsp
  hazelnuts
Cinnamon for
  sprinkling

1. Peel the banana, mash thoroughly and sweeten with honey.
2. Transfer to a high-sided bowl and beat in the buttermilk.
3. Pour into two glasses and sprinkle with the nuts and a little cinnamon.
(Photo top)

Preparation time: 10 mins
Serves 2
Approx. 180 kcal/755 kJ

Tip
The drink, including the hazelnuts, can be whizzed to a purée in a blender and sprinkled with cinnamon on top.

Cream Ice with Blueberries

Ingredients   Metric/Imperial

Double cream   150 ml/¼ pt
Water   100ml/3½floz
Acacia honey   30 ml/6 tsp
Egg yolks   2
Raisins   50 g/2 oz
Fresh or frozen   200 g/7 oz
  blueberries

1. Mix the cream well with the water and honey.
2. Beat the egg yolks in a bowl until creamy, add the cream and honey mixture and beat thoroughly.
3. Place the bowl in a second bowl, filled with hottish water, then whisk until thick. Stir in the raisins. Cool the mixture in a bowl of chilled water.
4. Leave until completely cold then beat until smooth. Cover the bowl and leave in the freezer for 2-3 hours, stirring the ice cream from time to time.
5. Accompany the ice cream with the berries, thawed if frozen.
(Photo bottom)

Preparation time: 15 mins
Freezing time: 2-3 hrs
Serves 2
Approx. 495 kcal/2080 kJ

Coppa Banana

Ingredients	Metric/Imperial
Ripe bananas	2
Unwhipped double cream	100 g/3½ fl oz
Water	150 ml/¼ pt
Glucose syrup	20 ml/4 tsp
Vanilla essence	5 ml/1 tsp
Whipped cream	20 ml/4 tsp
Chopped almonds	10 ml/2 tsp

1. Peel the bananas, chop the flesh and place in a blender.
2. Add the unwhipped cream, water, syrup and vanilla essence.
3. Blend to a smooth purée then place in a bowl. Cover tightly and freeze for 2-3 hours, whisking gently from time to time.
4. Put the ice cream into dessert glasses, put a blob of cream on each and sprinkle with almonds.
(Photo top)

Preparation time: 15 mins
Freezing time: 2-3 hrs
Serves 2
Approx. 400 kcal/1679 kJ

Blueberry Mix

Ingredients	Metric/Imperial
Crushed ice cubes	2
Buttermilk	300 ml/½ pt
Fresh or frozen blueberries	100 g/4 oz
Glucose syrup	10 ml/4 tsp

1. Put the crushed ice, buttermilk and blueberries into a blender, and blend to a purée.
2. Sweeten the drink with syrup and pour into two tall glasses.
(Photo bottom)

Preparation time: 5 mins
Serves 2
Approx. 135 kcal/565 kJ

Apple Cake

Ingredients Metric/Imperial

For the dough:

Butter, melted	150 g/5 oz
Honey	100 g/4 oz
Quark (20% fat)	250 g/9 oz
Grated lemon rind	10 ml/2 tsp
Egg yolk	1
Pinch of sea salt	
Baking powder	10 ml/2 tsp
Wholemeal flour	350 g/12 oz
Butter for greasing	

For the filling:

Soft dessert apples	800 g/1¾ lb
Raisins	100 g/4 oz

For the icing:

Butter	100 g/4 oz
Honey	100 g/4 oz
Cinnamon	8 ml/1½ tsp
Whipping cream	200 ml/7 fl oz

In addition:

Flaked almonds	100 g/4 oz

1. Mix the melted butter to a smooth cream with the honey and quark. Add the lemon rind, egg yolk and a good pinch of sea salt. Mix well.

2. Mix the baking powder with the flour and gradually stir into the quark mixture to form a pliable dough.

3. Spread the dough on a greased baking tray and leave to stand for about 15 minutes.

4. In the meantime, prepare the filling. Peel the apples, remove the cores and cut the flesh into thin slices.

5. Spread the slices over the dough, overlapping each other and sprinkling with the raisins.

6. Pre-heat the oven to 160°C/325°F/gas mark 3.

7. To make the icing, melt the butter in a pan. Add the honey, cinnamon and cream and whisk until fluffy.

8. Spoon the icing over the apples and sprinkle with the almond flakes. Bake for about 40 minutes.

Preparation time: 1 hr
Baking time: 40 mins
Makes 20 pieces
Approx. 295 kcal/1235 kJ

Quark Stollen

Ingredients	Metric/Imperial
Wholemeal flour	500 g/1 lb 2 oz
Cold butter	125 g/4½ oz
Baking powder	20 ml/4 tbsp
Pinch of sea salt	
Grated rind of lemon	½
Ground cardamom	5 ml/1 tsp
Ground mace or nutmeg	2.5 ml/½ tsp
Egg yolk	1
Currants	125 g/4½ oz
Raisins	125 g/4½ oz
Quark (20% fat)	250 g/9 oz
Vanilla essence	5 ml/1 tsp
Honey	150 g/5 oz
Almonds, coarsely chopped	125 g/4½ oz
Melted butter for brushing	
Butter for greasing	

1. Place about one-third of the flour on a work surface, make a hollow in the centre and fill with flakes of cold butter.

2. Add the baking powder, salt, grated lemon rind, the cardamom, mace or nutmeg and the egg yolk. Fork together to form crumbles.

3. Pre-heat the oven to 160°C/325°F/gas mark 3.

Wash the currants and raisins, dry thoroughly and mix with the quark.

4. Stir in the vanilla essence with the honey and almonds. Mix well. Add the flour crumble a little at a time and work to a firm dough.

5. Shape the dough into an elongated oval and transfer it to a greased baking tray. Brush with butter and bake the stollen for 50-60 minutes.

Preparation time: 15 mins
Baking time: 50-60 mins
Makes 15 pieces
Approx. 300 kcal/1250 kJ

Quark Crumb Cake

Ingredients Metric/Imperial

For the dough:

Fresh yeast	25 g/1 oz
Warm water	125 ml/4 fl oz
Wholemeal flour	250 g/9 oz
Butter, melted	30 g/1¼ oz
Honey	20 ml/4 tsp
Pinch of sea salt	
Butter for greasing	

For the crumbs:

Wholemeal flour	200 g/7 oz
Cold butter	100 g/4 oz
Honey	100 g/4 oz

For the filling:

Powdered gelatine	25 ml/4 tsp
Cold water	30 ml/2 tbsp
Quark (20% fat)	450 g/1 lb
Glucose syrup	100ml/3½floz
Vanilla essence	5 ml/ 1 tsp
Grated rind of lemon	1
Whipping cream	300 ml/½ pt

1. Dissolve the yeast in the warm water and work to a smooth dough with half the wholemeal flour. Leave to rise for 20 minutes in a warm place.
2. Add the rest of the wholemeal flour, the lukewarm butter, the honey and the sea salt. Knead to a pliable dough.
3. Grease a baking tin and spread the dough evenly over the base. Leave it, covered, in a warm place until the dough has doubled in size.
4. In the meantime pre-heat the oven to 160°C/325°F/gas mark 3.
5. To make the crumbs, fork together the flour, butter and the honey. Lay baking paper on to a baking tray and spread the crumbs on top. Bake for 20 minutes and leave to cool.
6. Place the baking tin with the dough into the oven and bake for 25 minutes. (In a fan oven both crumbs and dough can be baked at the same time.) Leave the dough to cool as well.
7. To make the filling, soak the gelatine in cold water for about 10 minutes then melt over a low heat and leave to cool.
8. In the meantime, whisk the quark until smooth and sweeten with the syrup. Stir in the vanilla and lemon rind.
9. Whip the cream until stiff and fold it carefully into the quark mixture. Fold in the liquid gelatine a little at a time.
10. Leave the topping in the cool until it just begins to solidify, then spread over the cooked dough to form a thick layer.
11. Finally sprinkle the wholemeal crumbs on top of the cake and leave to stand for at least 20 minutes until cold before cutting — longer if possible to give the gelatine mixture time to set as firmly as possible. *(Photo opposite top)*

Preparation time: 1½ hours
Baking time: 45 mins
Makes 15 pieces
Approx. 300 kcal/1250 kJ

Honey Bars

Ingredients Metric/Imperial

Butter	250 g/9 oz
Clear honey	500 g/1 lb 2oz
Cream	45 ml/3 tbsp
Rum	45 ml/3 tbsp
Ground almonds	250 g/9 oz
Grated rind of lemon	1
Cinnamon	20 ml/4 tsp
Wholemeal flour	500 g/1 lb 2oz
Millet flour	250 g/9 oz
Butter for greasing	

1. Melt the butter over a gentle heat, whisking gently.
2. Gradually add the honey, cream, rum, almonds, grated lemon rind and the cinnamon. Stir thoroughly to mix.
3. Mix the wholemeal and millet flours together and knead to a smooth and pliable dough with the butter mixture.
4. Leave the dough to rise for about 10 minutes. Pre-heat the oven to 150°C/300°F/gas mark 2.
5. In the meantime, grease a baking tin with the butter, add the dough and spread out 1 cm/½ in in thickness.
6. Transfer to the oven and bake for 20 minutes.
7. Whilst still warm, cut the dough into 1 × 4 cm (½ × 1½ in) bars. Leave to cool then store in a biscuit tin. Leave for three to four days before eating to allow flavours to develop. *(Photo opposite bottom)*

Preparation time: 1 hr
Baking time: 20 mins
Makes 80
Approx. 95 kcal/395 kJ

Wholemeal Cinnamon Biscuits

Ingredients	Metric/Imperial
Wholemeal flour	200 g/7 oz
Pinch of sea salt	
Ground cardamom	5 ml/1 tsp
Cinnamon	5 ml/1 tsp
Ground cloves	5 ml/1 tsp
Egg yolk	1
Cold butter	125 g/4 oz
Ground almonds, cut into flakes	100 g/3 oz
Clear honey	75 g/3 oz
Butter for greasing	

1. In a fairly large bowl, mix the flour with the salt and spices.
2. Make a hollow in the centre and drop in the egg yolk and butter. Add the almonds and honey. Knead fairly quickly into a pliable dough.
3. Roll out on a floured surface to about 5 mm/ ¼ in thick then cut into rounds with a pastry cutter. Pre-heat the oven to 180°C/350°F/gas mark 4.
4. Arrange the biscuits on a greased baking tray and bake for about 10 minutes. Cool on a wire rack.
(Photo opposite bottom)

Preparation time: 45 mins
Baking time: 10 mins
Makes 30
Approx. 85 kcal/355 kJ

Tip
It is much easier to roll out the dough if a piece of cling film is placed between the rolling pin and the dough.

Oat Flake Medallions

Ingredients	Metric/Imperial
Rolled oats	150 g/5 oz
Wholemeal flour	100 g/4 oz
Baking powder	5 ml/1 tsp
Cold butter	125 g/4½ oz
Clear honey	125 g/4½ oz
Grated rind of lemon	½
Ground almonds	50 g/2 oz
Sesame seeds	50 g/2 oz
Butter for greasing	

1. Tip the oats into a large bowl.
2. Mix in the flour and baking powder and run the ingredients through your fingers until well mixed.
3. Grate in the butter. Add the honey, lemon rind, almonds and sesame seeds. Knead lightly together to form a pliable dough.
4. Pre-heat the oven to 160°C/325°F/gas mark 3. Shape the dough into a roll about 4 cm/1½ in in diameter then cut into 1 cm/½ in slices.
5. Place on to a buttered baking tray, leaving space around each as they spread a little while cooking. Bake the biscuits for about 10 minutes then cool on a wire rack.
(Photo opposite top)

Preparation time: 35 mins
Baking time: 10 mins
Makes 30
Approx. 95 kcal/400 kJ

Almond Biscuits

Ingredients	Metric/Imperial
Wholemeal flour	200 g/7 oz
Baking powder	5 ml/1 tsp
Butter	75 g/3 oz
Water	30 ml/6 tsp
Vanilla essence	5 ml/1 tsp
Whipping Cream	10 ml/2 tsp
Ground almonds	100 g/4 oz
Clear honey	75 g/3 oz
Butter for greasing	
Whipped cream for spreading	
Almond halves	30

1. Tip the flour and baking powder into a bowl.
2. Add the water, vanilla essence, cream, ground almonds and honey and quickly work to a pliable dough.
3. Shape into a roll about 4 cm/1½ in in diameter, wrap in foil and leave to stand for an hour in a cool place.
4. Pre-heat the oven to 180°C/350°F/gas mark 4. Cut the roll into 1 cm/ ½ in thick slices and transfer to a buttered baking tray.
5. Brush the biscuits with a little cream and top each half with an almond. Bake for 10-12 minutes then cool on a wire rack.
(Photo opposite centre)

Preparation time: 45 mins
Cooling time: 1 hr
Baking time: 10 mins
Makes 30
Approx. 79 kcal/330 kJ

Four Corn Biscuits

Ingredients Metric/Imperial

For the dough:

Cracked wheat	100 g/4 oz
Wholemeal flour	100 g/4 oz
Oat flour	100 g/4 oz
Millet flour	75 g/3 oz
Cold butter	200 g/7 oz
Pinch of sea salt	
Grated rind of lemon	1
Egg yolk	½
Honey	150 g/5 oz

In addition:

Butter for greasing	
Almonds, halved	20

1. Tip all the flours into a bowl then grate in the butter.

2. Add the salt, lemon rind, egg yolk and honey and knead to a soft, pliable pastry, similar to shortcrust.

3. Pre-heat the oven to 160°C/325°F/gas mark 3. Roll out the dough to 5 mm/¼ in in thickness between two sheets of cling film and cut the dough into about 40 squares with a sharp knife.

4. Transfer the biscuits to a buttered baking tray and top each with an almond half. Bake the biscuits for 8-10 minutes then cool on a wire rack.

(Photo bottom)

Preparation time: 45 mins
Baking time: 8-10 mins
Makes 40
Approx. 84 kcal/350 kJ

Sesame Sticks

Ingredients Metric/Imperial

For the dough:

Wholemeal flour	250 g/9 oz
Baking powder	8 ml/1½ tsp
Herb salt	5 ml/1 tsp
Cold pressed sunflower oil	30 ml/2 tsp
Buttermilk	200 ml/7 fl oz

In addition:

Sesame seeds	45 ml/3 tbsp
Butter for greasing	

1. Tip the flour into a bowl then toss in the baking powder and herb salt.

2. Add the sunflower oil and buttermilk and knead to a smooth and pliable dough.

3. Divide the dough into 30 equal-sized pieces and roll them into 10 cm/4 in long sticks. Coat all over with sesame seeds and press lightly into the dough. Transfer to a buttered baking tray.

4. Cover the sticks and place in the refrigerator for about 1 hour. Pre-heat the oven to 180°C/350°F/ gas mark 4 and bake for 15-18 minutes. Cool on a wire rack.

(Photo centre right)

Preparation time: 45 mins
Cooling time: 1 hr
Baking time: 18 mins
Makes 30
Approx. 45 kcal/190 kJ

Savoury Cheese Biscuits

Ingredients	Metric/Imperial
Wholemeal flour	125 g/4½ oz
Gouda or Cheddar cheese, grated	75g /3 oz
Butter	50 g/2 oz
Single cream	50 ml/2 fl oz

In addition:

Egg yolk	1
Water	10 ml/2 tsp
Caraway, sesame or poppy seeds	

1. Tip the flour into a bowl. Add the cheese, butter and cream and work into a pliable dough. Transfer to a floured surface.

2. Shape into a roll about 3 cm/1½ in in diameter. Wrap in cling film and refrigerate for 1 hour.

3. Cut the roll into about 35 slices and place on a buttered baking tray. Pre-heat the oven to 180°C/350°F/gas mark 4.

4. Whisk the egg yolk with water and use to brush tops of biscuits. Sprinkle with either caraway seeds, sesame seeds or poppy seeds and bake for 18 minutes. Cool on a wire rack.

(Photo top)

Preparation time: 45 mins
Cooling time: 1 hr
Baking time: 18 mins
Makes 35
Approx. 40 kcal/165 kJ

Pineapple Yoghurt

Ingredients	Metric/Imperial
Fresh pineapple	¼
Natural yoghurt (3.5% fat)	150 ml/¼ pt
Glucose syrup	10 ml/2 tsp
Lemon balm leaves	3 small

1. Peel the pineapple and remove the brown 'eyes' with the tip of a potato peeler. Cut the fruit into small pieces, saving all the juice.
2. Beat the yoghurt until creamy, sweeten with syrup then add the pineapple pieces and juice. Garnish with the lemon balm leaves and eat immediately.
(Photo opposite centre left)

Preparation time: 20 mins
Serves 1
Approx. 205 kcal/860 kJ

Strawberry Quark

Ingredients	Metric/Imperial
Strawberries	250 g/9 oz
Glucose syrup	30 ml/2 tbsp
Quark (20% fat)	250 g/9 oz
Sesame seeds	10 ml/2 tsp

1. Put aside about two of the best strawberries for decoration. Work remainder to a fine purée.
2. Sweeten with the syrup and combine with the quark.

3. Transfer to two dessert dishes, sprinkle with sesame seeds and top with strawberries.
(Photo opposite centre right)

Preparation time: 15 mins
Serves 2
Approx. 250 kcal/1045 kJ

Grapefruit with Soft Cheese

Ingredients	Metric/Imperial
Pink grapefruit	1
Glucose syrup	10 ml/2 tsp
Cottage cheese	150 g/5 oz
Mint leaves	4

1. Halve the grapefruit. Remove the flesh from both halves and cut into small pieces, saving the juice.

2. Mix the grapefruit juice thoroughly with the syrup.
3. Combine the cottage cheese with the sweetened juice and stir in the pieces of grapefruit.
4. Spoon into the empty grapefruit halves then decorate with mint leaves.

(Photo opposite bottom)

Preparation time: 10 mins
Serves 2
Approx. 150 kcal/640 kJ

Filled Grapefruit

Ingredients	Metric/Imperial
Pink grapefruit	1
Cottage cheese	150 g/5 oz
Roast beef	50 g/2 oz
Small dill sprigs	2

1. Halve the grapefruit. Remove the flesh from both halves and cut into small pieces, saving the juice.
2. Combine the grapefruit pieces and juice with the cottage cheese and spoon into the empty grapefruit halves.

3. Cut the beef into small strips, arrange over the grapefruit and garnish with the dill.
(Photo opposite top)

Preparation time: 10 mins
Serves 2
Approx. 160 kcal/680 kJ

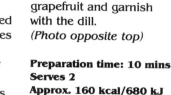

Strawberry Drink

Ingredients	Metric/Imperial
Strawberries	100 g/4 oz
Glucose syrup	10 ml/2 tsp
Drinking yoghurt, flavour to taste	250 g/9 oz

1. Purée the strawberries and sweeten with the syrup.
2. Add the yoghurt a little at a time and mix well. Pour into a glass for serving.
(Photo opposite top)

Preparation time: 10 mins
Serves 1
Approx. 225 kcal/940 kJ

Variations
Depending on the time of year, the drink can be made with other fruits such as oranges, blueberries, mango, blackcurrants, blackberries.

Vitamin C Bombe

Ingredients Metric/Imperial

Blood oranges	2
Kiwis	2
Quark (20% fat)	125 g/4½ oz
Glucose syrup	20 ml/4 tsp
Chopped almonds to garnish	20 ml/4 tsp

1. Cut the peel and the white skin away from the oranges, leaving them whole.

2. With a sharp knife, cut out segments and fruit from in between the fibrous membranes. Cut into small pieces. What is left should be squeezed by hand over a bowl to collect the juice.
3. Peel the kiwis, cut into slices and mix with the orange segments.

4. Mix the squeezed orange juice with the quark and sweeten with the syrup.
5. Divide the fruit between two dishes, top with the quark mixture, then sprinkle with nuts.
(Photo centre left)

Preparation time: 20 mins
Serves 2
Approx. 250 kcal/1050 kJ

Tip
Put the quark on to the fruit just before serving, as it will become bitter quickly when mixed with fresh kiwis.

Pineapple Dessert

Ingredients Metric/Imperial

Desiccated coconut	20 ml/4 tsp
Fresh peeled pineapple	2 slices
Whipped cream	20 ml/4 tsp

1. Lightly dry roast the coconut in a non-stick frying pan, turning frequently.
2. Coat the pineapple slices with the coconut and arrange on a plate. Decorate with the whipped cream.
(Photo bottom)

Preparation time: 10 mins
Serves 1
Approx. 215 kcal/910 kJ

Melon Cocktail

Ingredients	Metric/Imperial
Raisins	20 ml/4 tsp
Dash of gin	1
Ripe melon	1
Large orange	1
Seasonal fruit (strawberries, raspberries, nectarines)	250 g/9 oz
Juice of lemon	½
Glucose syrup	10 ml/2 tsp
Sprig of mint	1

1. Sprinkle the raisins with gin and leave to soak for two hours.
2. Cut the melon in half and remove the seeds. Reserve the halves. Cut the flesh into small balls with a melon baller.
3. Divide the orange into segments (see picture on page 42). What is left should be squeezed over a bowl to collect the juice.
4. Mix the orange segments with the melon balls. Add seasonal fruit as desired, first cut up into small pieces.
5. Mix the lemon juice with the reserved orange juice and sweeten with the syrup. Add to the fruit mixture with raisins.
6. Fill the melon halves with the fruit and decorate with mint leaves. Chill thoroughly before serving.
(Photo top right)

Marinating time: 2 hrs
Preparation time: 25 mins
plus cooling
Serves 4
Approx. 105 kcal/435 kJ

Fruity Buttermilk Dessert

Ingredients	Metric/Imperial
Powdered gelatine	20 ml/4 tsp
Cold water	30 ml/2 tbsp
Strawberries	300 g/11 oz
Buttermilk	300 ml/½ pt
Glucose syrup	50 ml/2 fl oz
Strawberries for garnishing	6

1. Leave the gelatine to soak for about 10 minutes in the cold water.
2. Meanwhile, purée the strawberries, combine with the buttermilk and syrup.
3. Dissolve gelatine in a saucepan over a low heat. Pour gradually into the buttermilk mixture and mix well in. Spoon into glasses and leave to set in the refrigerator. Decorate with fresh strawberries.
(Photo top left)

Preparation time: 25 mins
Serves 2
Approx. 235 kcal/985 kJ

Middle European Iced Cherry Soup

Ingredients	Metric/Imperial
Morello cherries or drained and stoned bottled ones	500 g/1 lb 2 oz
Cold water	300 ml/½ pt
Cinnamon stick	1
Cloves	3
Arrowroot	15 ml/1 tbsp
Cold water	15 ml/1 tbsp
Glucose syrup	30 ml/2 tbsp

1. Stone the cherries and tip into a saucepan. Add the water, cinnamon and the cloves.
2. Bring slowly to the boil then simmer, uncovered, for 3-4 minutes. Mix the arrowroot with cold water, stir until smooth then gradually add to the soup. Reboil, stirring all the time, and simmer until the soup is clear. Discard the cinnamon and cloves.
3. Sweeten with syrup, then leave to cool. Cover, chill and serve.
(Photo left)

Preparation time: 25 mins plus cooling
Serves 2
Approx. 205 kcal/860 kJ

Raspberry Sorbet

Ingredients	Metric/Imperial
Fresh or deep frozen raspberries	200 g/7 oz
Thick Greek yoghurt	175 ml/6 fl oz
Glucose syrup	
Lemon juice	30 ml/2 tbsp
Raspberries for garnish	10 ml/2 tsp

1. Purée the fresh or defrosted raspberries in a blender then sieve to remove the seeds.
2. Combine with the remaining ingredients.
3. Transfer to a bowl, cover closely and freeze for 2-3 hours, beating the sorbet every 20 minutes for smoothness.
4. Scoop into two dishes, garnish with raspberries and serve while still icy cold.
(Photo centre)

Preparation time: 20 mins
Freezing time: 2-3 hrs
Serves 2
Approx. 150 kcal/620 kJ

Berry Dessert

Ingredients	Metric/Imperial
Seasonal or selection of deep frozen berries	200 g/7 oz
Glucose syrup	150 ml/¼ pt
Lemon juice	20 ml/4 tsp
Arrowroot	10 ml/2 tsp
Cold water	10 ml/2 tsp
Whipped cream	15 ml/1 tbsp

1. Mix the fresh or defrosted fruit with the water, then pass through a strainer to extract the juice. Sweeten with syrup then add the lemon juice. Bring the mixture to boil in a saucepan
2. Add the arrowroot smoothly blended with water and bring to the boil, stirring. Simmer for 2 minutes then leave to cool to lukewarm. Spoon into a dish and garnish with cream.
(Photo top)

Preparation time: 20 mins plus cooling
Serves 1
Approx. 225 kcal/935 kJ

Starters, Salads and Soups

Many recipes for crispy, crunchy salads and delicous soups are designed to bring pleasure to your everyday cooking. The colours in which the titles are printed are to assist you to combine foods properly: red with red, blue with blue, grey with either.

One of the most important things to remember in combining foods is to eat plenty of fresh vegetables. If, before your midday meal, you eat a large salad, you are taking a step in the right direction, bearing in mind how rich in vitamins, minerals and fibre vegetables are with the added plus of being low in calories. A salad eaten before the main meal will fill you up and this is something that all those who need to watch their figure should remember.

Mixed Bean Sprout Salad

Ingredients Metric/Imperial

Chinese cabbage	250 g/9 oz
Mushrooms	150 g/5 oz
Soy bean sprouts	150 g/5 oz
Tomatoes	3

For the dressing:

Soy sauce	10 ml/2 tsp
Soured cream	45 ml/3 tbsp
Cold water	30 ml/2 tbsp
Herb salt	5 ml/1 tsp
Chopped mixed herbs (basil, parsley, sorrel)	15 ml/1 tbsp
Cold pressed sunflower oil	10 ml/2 tsp

In addition:

| Walnuts | 5 |
| Fresh herbs for garnish (optional) | |

1. Cut the Chinese cabbage into strips and slice the mushrooms.
2. Wash the soy bean sprouts carefully and leave to drain.
3. Cut each tomato into 8 pieces and mix with the prepared vegetables and bean sprouts.
4. Stir together with soy sauce, soured cream, water and the herb salt. Beat in the herbs and the oil and pour the dressing over the salad. Place the walnuts on top or chop and sprinkle. Garnish with herb sprigs, if using.
(Photo top right)

Preparation time: 25 mins
Serves 2
Approx. 215 kcal/900 kJ

Summer Salad with Sprouts

Ingredients Metric/Imperial

Cucumber	½
Small onion	1
Tomatoes	3
Mung or soy bean sprouts	150 g/5 oz
Frozen sweet corn, thawed	45 ml/3 tbsp

For the dressing:

Soured thick cream milk	150 g/5 oz
Cold water	10 ml/2 tsp
Soy sauce	10 ml/2 tsp
Curry powder	5 ml/1 tsp
Herb salt	5 ml/1 tsp

In addition:

| Small dill sprigs | 3 |

1. Peel the cucumber, quarter it lengthways and cut into pieces.
2. Peel the onion and cut into rings.
3. Dice the tomato flesh.
4. Wash the mung or soy bean sprouts well, leave to drain and toss with the sweet corn and cucumber.
5. Mix in the onion rings and tomatoes.
6. Combine all ingredients for the dressing, beating well. Pour over the salad and garnish with dill.
(Photo top left)

Preparation time: 25 mins
Serves 2
Approx. 210 kcal/865 kJ

Italian Salad

Ingredients	Metric/Imperial
Small iceberg lettuce	1
Tomatoes	3
Onion	1
Cucumber	1

For the dressing:

Soy sauce	10 ml/2 tsp
Lemon juice	10 ml/2 tsp
Cold pressed olive oil	10 ml/2 tsp
Herb salt	8 ml/1½ tsp
Olives preserved in oil with garlic and chopped	10
Skimmed milk	60 ml/4 tbsp

In addition:

Chopped fresh herbs (dill, basil, parsley)	30 ml/2 tbsp

1. Clean the lettuce and tear the leaves into pieces.
2. Wash and dry the tomatoes and dice the flesh.
3. Peel the onions and cut into thin slices then separate the slices into rings.
4. Peel the cucumber, cut into 4 strips lengthways, remove the seeds and cut the remainder into pieces about 1 cm/½ in thick. Toss all the prepared ingredients together.
5. To make the dressing, whisk all the ingredients well together.
6. Toss with the salad ingredients then garnish with herbs.
(Photo bottom)

Preparation time: 15 mins
Serves 2
Approx. 145 kcal/615 kJ

Waldeck Salad

Ingredients Metric/Imperial

Mixed vegetables made up of 16 types:	*800 g/1¾ lb*

Carrots, cucumber, tomato, mushrooms, cauliflower, radishes, pepper, fennel, onion, iceberg lettuce, radicchio. courgettes, soy bean sprouts, white cabbage, kohlrabi and horseradish or frisée

For the dressing:

Fromage frais	*175 ml/6 fl oz*
Full cream milk	*100ml/3½ fl oz*
Soy sauce	*15 ml/1 tbsp*
Herb salt	*10 ml/2 tsp*
Glucose syrup	*10 ml/2 tsp*
Cold pressed olive oil to taste	*10 ml/2 tsp*
Garlic clove, peeled and crushed	*1*
Chopped fresh herbs (basil, parsley)	*30 ml/2 tbsp*

1. Chop the vegetables fairly finely and transfer to a large bowl.
2. Mix all the dressing ingredients well together. Pour over the salad and toss thoroughly.
(Photo opposite top)

Preparation time: 40 mins
Serves 4
Approx. 105 kcal/440 kJ

Beetroot Salad

Ingredients Metric/Imperial

Cooked beetroots	*600 g/ 1¼-1½ lb*

For the dressing:

Soy sauce	*10 ml/2 tsp*
Cold water	*60 ml/4 tbsp*
Soured cream	*30 ml/6 tsp*
Herb salt	*5 ml/1 tsp*
Caraway seeds	*5 ml/1 tsp*
Cold pressed sunflower oil	*10 ml/2 tsp*
Small onion	*1*

In addition:

Chopped fresh parsley	*20 ml/4 tsp*

1. Skin the beetroots and cut flesh into small dice.
2. To make the dressing, whisk all the ingredients well together except the onion.
3. Peel the onion, dice finely and add to the dressing. Combine with the diced beetroot and sprinkle parsley over the top.
(Photo opposite centre)

Preparation time: 45 mins
Serves 2
Approx. 210 kcal/885 kJ

Raw Vegetables with Nuts

Ingredients Metric/Imperial

Bunch radishes 1	
Small Lollo rosso lettuce	*1*
Soy bean sprouts	*100 g/4 oz*

For the dressing:

Small onion	*1*
Soy sauce	*10 ml/2 tsp*
Cold water	*30 ml/2 tbsp*
Herb salt	*5 ml/1 tsp*
Cold pressed sunflower oil	*10 ml/2 tsp*

In addition:

Chopped almonds	*20 ml/ 4 tsp*

1. Clean the radishes and cut into fine chips.
2. Clean the Lollo rosso and tear the leaves into pieces.
3. Wash the soy bean sprouts, sort through, remove any damaged ones and leave to drain. Mix all the prepared ingredients together.
4. Peel the onion and dice finely. Keep on one side.
5. For the dressing, beat all the ingredients well together and add to the salad with the onion. Sprinkle with almonds to garnish.
(Photo opposite bottom)

Preparation time: 25 mins
Serves 1-2
Approx. 75 kcal/325 kJ

Mexican Bean Salad

Ingredients	Metric/Imperial
Green beans	350 g/12 oz
Sea salt	
Sprig of fresh savoury	1
Tomatoes	3
Mushrooms	100 g/4 oz
Shallots	2
Frozen sweet corn, thawed	100 g/4 oz

For the dressing:

Soy sauce	10 ml/2 tsp
Cold water	60 ml/4 tbsp
Cold pressed sunflower oil	10 ml/2 tsp
Whipping cream	50 g/2 oz
Herb salt	
Finely chopped fresh chives	30 ml/2 tbsp

1. Cut the beans into pieces about 4 cm/1½ in long. Cook in lightly salted water.
2. Meanwhile, wash and dry tomatoes and cut the flesh into pieces.
3. Wipe the mushrooms with a damp cloth and slice thinly. Peel the shallots and chop finely.
4. Mix together all the dressing ingredients.
5. Drain the beans. Combine with all the prepared ingredients including the sweet corn. Leave the salad to stand for about 30 minutes before serving.
(Photo top)

Preparation time: 45 mins
Marinating time: 30 mins
Serves 2
Approx. 270 kcal/1130 kJ

Bavarian Caraway Cabbage

Ingredients	Metric/Imperial
Small white cabbage	400 g/14 oz
Sea salt	5 ml/1 tsp
Onion	1
Cold pressed sunflower oil	10 ml/2 tsp
Paprika	5 ml/1 tsp
Soy sauce	10 ml/2 tsp
Cold water	60 ml/4 tbsp
Caraway seeds	5 ml/1 tsp

1. Remove and discard the hard outer leaves from the cabbage and cut into narrow strips, removing tough pieces of stalk.
2. Put the cabbage into a large bowl and toss with the salt.
3. Dice the onion finely and add to the cabbage with the oil and paprika. Bring the soy sauce, water and caraway seeds to the boil and pour over the cabbage. Leave to stand for 1-2 hours until cool before serving.
(Photo centre)

Preparation time: 20 mins
Marinating time: 1 hr
Serves 2
Approx. 215 kcal/900 kJ

Raw Cauliflower Salad

Ingredients	Metric/Imperial
Cauliflower	400 g/14 oz
Green peppers	2
Firm tomatoes	4
Onion	1

For the dressing:

Soy sauce	10 ml/2 tsp
Cold pressed sunflower oil	10 ml/2 tsp
Glucose syrup	10 ml/2 tsp
Single cream	30 ml/2 tbsp
Garlic clove, peeled and crushed	1
Paprika	5 ml/1 tsp
Herb salt	20 ml/4 tsp
Chopped fresh chives	

1. Chop the cauliflower coarsely. Halve the peppers, remove the seeds and chop. Cut the tomatoes into pieces.
2. Dice the onion finely and mix with the prepared vegetables.
3. Beat together all the dressing ingredients except the chives, then toss with the vegetables.
4. Sprinkle with the chives to garnish.
(Photo bottom)

Preparation time: 20 mins
Serves 2
Approx. 215 kcal/885 kJ

Fennel Salad with Fruit

Ingredients Metric/Imperial

Fennel bulbs	2
Chicory heads	2
Large crisp apple	1
Lemon juice	10 ml/2 tsp
Pink grapefruit	1

For the dressing:

Yellow grapefruit	1
Single cream	100ml/3½floz
Glucose syrup	10 ml/2 tsp
Pinch of cayenne pepper	
Sea salt	5 ml/1 tsp

In addition:

Flaked almond	15 ml/1 tbsp

1. Clean the fennel, remove the green leaves then cut each bulb lengthways into thin strips. Chop up the green leaves and leave on one side.

2. Halve the chicory lengthways, remove the bitter stalk, then cut the leaves into strips about 1 cm/½ in wide. Mix with the fennel strips.

3. Halve the apple, remove the core and cut flesh into thin segments. Sprinkle with the lemon juice.

4. Peel the pink grapefruit and remove the pith. Cut out the flesh between the fibrous segments and put into a bowl. Reserve the juice by squeezing what is left of the fruit and add to the bowl of grapefruit with all the prepared vegetables.

5. For the dressing, squeeze the juice out of the second grapefruit and mix with all the remaining ingredients.

6. Add to the prepared ingredients and toss well to mix. Garnish with the green fennel leaves and the flaked almonds.

Preparation time: 25 mins
Serves 2
Approx. 440 kcal/1855 kJ

Fruity Raw Food Platter

Ingredients	Metric/Imperial
Ripe pear	1
Honeydew melon	½
Palm heart (canned) or courgette	1
Iceberg lettuce	½
Almonds	10

For the dressing:

Lemon juice	10 ml/2 tsp
Cold water	45 ml/3 tbsp
Sea salt	3 ml/½ tsp
Glucose syrup	5 ml/1 tsp
Cold pressed sunflower oil	10 ml/2 tsp

In addition:
Finely chopped 20 ml/4 tsp fresh dill

1. Quarter the pear and remove the core. Cut the flesh into small pieces.
2. Remove the seeds from the melon, remove the flesh and cut into dice.
3. Thinly slice the palm heart or courgette.
4. Wash and drain the lettuce and tear into small pieces.
5. Chop the almonds coarsely. Mix all the prepared ingredients well together in a large bowl.
6. For the dressing, whisk all the ingredients until evenly blended then pour over salad. Toss well to mix then sprinkle with dill.

Preparation time: 20 mins
Serves 2
Approx. 310 kcal/1310 kJ

Fennel and Celery Salad

Ingredients	Metric/Imperial
Fennel bulb	1
Celeriac	125 g/4½ oz
Cooking apples	2
Lemon juice	10 ml/2 tsp
Orange	1

For the dressing:

Orange	1
Pinch of cayenne pepper	1
Glucose syrup	10 ml/2 tsp
Herb salt	5 ml/1 tsp
Soured cream	30 ml/2 tbsp
Raisins	25 ml/1 oz
Chopped almonds	10 ml/2 tsp

1. Cut each fennel along its length into thin strips.
2. Peel and grate the celeriac.
3. Quarter the apples, remove the cores and cut the apples into thin segments. Combine all the prepared ingredients in a bowl and sprinkle with lemon juice to prevent browning.
4. Peel the orange and remove the pith. Cut out the segments of flesh in between the fibrous dividers and add to the bowl of salad ingredients.
5. To make the dressing, squeeze the second orange and beat with the rest of the dressing ingredients, except the raisins and almonds.
6. Pour the dressing over the salad, toss well and sprinkle with raisins and almonds. Leave to stand for about 30 minutes before serving.
(Photo bottom)

Preparation time: 45 mins
Marinating time: 30 mins
Serves 2
Approx. 275 kcal/1145 kJ

Carrot and Pear Salad

Ingredients	Metric/Imperial
Carrots	2
Pear	1
Lemon juice	10 ml/2 tsp

For the dressing:

Natural yoghurt (3.5% fat)	75 ml/5 tbsp
Single cream	20 ml/4 tsp
Glucose syrup	10 ml/2 tsp

In addition:

Coarsely chopped almonds	10 ml/2 tsp

1. Peel the carrots and cut into very fine strips.
2. Halve the pear, remove the core and dice the flesh finely. Mix with the carrot strips in a bowl and sprinkle with lemon juice.
3. Combine the yoghurt with the cream and syrup. Add to the carrots and pear and sprinkle with chopped almonds.
(Photo centre left)

Preparation time: 20 mins
Serves 1
Approx. 315 kcal/1320 kJ

Alpine Vegetable Cheese Salad

Ingredients	Metric/Imperial
Red pepper	1
Onion	1
Black olives	7
Tomatoes	2
Emmenthal cheese	50 g/2 oz

For the dressing:

Soy sauce	10 ml/2 tsp
Cold water	60 ml/4 tbsp
Single cream	45 ml/3 tbsp
Herb salt	5 ml/1 tsp
Glucose syrup	5 ml/1 tsp
Cold pressed olive oil	10 ml/2 tsp

In addition:

Chopped fresh chives	20 ml/4 tsp

1. Halve the pepper, remove inside fibres and seeds and cut the flesh into strips. Peel the onion, slice thinly and separate into rings.
2. Remove the stones from the olives. Cut the tomatoes into small dice.
3. Cut the cheese into strips, put into a large bowl and add all the prepared ingredients. Toss well.
4. For the dressing, whisk all the ingredients well together.
5. Pour the dressing over the salad, toss well to mix then sprinkle with chopped chives.
(Photo centre right)

Preparation time: 25 mins
Serves 1
Approx. 445 kcal/1865 kJ

Celeriac Salad

Ingredients	Metric/Imperial
Celeriac	125 g/4½ oz
Large cooking apples	2
Lemon juice	10 ml/2 tsp
Walnuts	6
Raisins	75 g/3 oz
Thick Greek yoghurt	175 ml/6 fl oz
Herb salt	5 ml/1 tsp

1. Peel the celeriac, then cut into fine chips or grate if preferred.
2. Quarter the apples, remove the cores then grate the flesh coarsely. Put into a bowl. Mix with the celeriac then sprinkle with the lemon juice.
3. Chop the walnuts coarsely and add to bowl with the raisins.
4. Toss with the yoghurt, seasoning with herb salt to taste.
(Photo top)

Preparation time: 25 mins
Serves 2
Approx. 295 kcal/1230 kJ

Pancake
Strip Soup

Ingredients Metric/Imperial

For the pancake strips:

Single cream	45 ml/3 tbsp
Cold water	120 ml/4 fl oz
Egg yolk	1
Sea salt	2.5 ml/½ tsp
Pinch of grated nutmeg	
Wholemeal flour	50 g/2 oz
Cold pressed sunflower oil	20 ml/4 tsp

For the soup:

Vegetable stock	600 ml/1 pt

In addition:

Chopped fresh chives	10 ml/2 tsp
Finely chopped fresh parsley	10 ml/2 tsp
Chopped fresh or dried lovage	5 ml/1 tsp

1. Whisk the cream with the water and egg yolk in a bowl until well combined. Season with the sea salt and nutmeg.

2. Gradually add to the flour, beating until the batter is smooth and creamy-looking.

3. Heat half the oil in a non-stick frying pan over a medium heat. Add half of the batter, spread evenly over base of pan to form a thin pancake and fry until both sides are brown. Repeat, using up the rest of the oil (for frying) and the batter.

4. Leave the pancakes to cool then cut into thin strips.

5. Heat up the vegetable stock and season with sea salt. Add the pancake strips, pour into bowls and sprinkle with herbs.

Preparation time: 15 mins
Serves 2
Approx. 315 kcal/1325 kJ

Paprika Cream Soup

Ingredients	Metric/Imperial
Onion	1
Red pepper	1
Yellow pepper	1
Butter	10 ml/2 tsp
Wholemeal flour	10 ml/2 tsp
Vegetable stock	450 ml/¾ pt
Single cream	30 ml/2 tbsp
Chopped fresh parsley	10 ml/2 tsp

1. Peel and finely chop the onion.
2. Halve the peppers, removing the inside fibres and seeds and cut the flesh into strips. Reserve a few strips for garnishing.
3. Gently cook the onion and pepper strips in butter in a saucepan for 5 minutes, stirring from time to time.
4. Sprinkle the wholemeal flour over the top and mix it well in. Gradually add the vegetable stock, stirring all the time.
5. Half cover and simmer for 10 minutes. Purée the soup, return to the saucepan and add the cream.
6. Stir in the reserved pepper strips, heat through then pour soup into bowls and sprinkle with parsley to serve.

Preparation time: 35 mins
Serves 2
Approx. 150 kcal/620 kJ

Vegetable Soup

Ingredients	Metric/Imperial
Small onion	1
Butter	5 ml/1 tsp
Carrot	1
Celeriac	75 g/3 oz
Small leek	1
Wholemeal flour	50 g/2 oz
Hot water	300 ml/¾ pt
Vegetable stock powder	10 ml/2 tsp
Single cream	20 ml/4 tsp
Chopped fresh parsley	20 ml/4 tsp

1. Peel the onion, dice finely and fry lightly in the butter in a saucepan.
2. Peel the carrot and the celeriac and finely chop. Clean the leek and cut into fine shreds. Add all three to the onions, then mix in the wholemeal flour, stirring continuously.
3. Add the water flavoured with the stock powder. Cover and simmer the soup for about 20 minutes.
4. Stir in the cream and sprinkle with parsley.
(Photo top)

Preparation time: 35 mins
Serves 1-2
Approx 335 kcal/1420 kJ

Millet Soup

Ingredients	Metric/Imperial
Millet	40 g/1½ oz
Vegetable stock	400 ml/14 fl oz
Small leek	1
Ground nutmeg	2.5 ml/½ tsp
Single cream	30 ml/2 tbsp
Chopped fresh chives	30 ml/2 tbsp

1. Rinse the millet with hot water and transfer to a saucepan with the vegetable stock. Cover and simmer over a low heat for about 15 minutes.
2. Meanwhile, clean the leek and cut into rings. Add to the pan, cover and cook for another 10 minutes.
3. Purée the soup then season with ground nutmeg. Stir in the cream, pour into bowls and sprinkle with chives.
(Photo centre)

Preparation time: 40 mins
Serves 1-2
Approx 180 kcal/755 kJ

Asparagus Soup

Ingredients	Metric/Imperial
Vegetable stock	400 ml/14 fl oz
Glucose syrup	2.5 ml/½ tsp
Asparagus	400 g/14 oz
Butter	10 ml/2 tsp
Wholemeal flour	20 ml/4 tsp
Whipping cream	20 ml/4 tsp
Chopped fresh parsley	10 ml/2 tsp

1. Bring stock to the boil then add the syrup. Leave over a minimal heat.
2. Peel the asparagus, cutting off the woody ends. Cut the sticks into pieces about 4 cm/1½ in long.
3. Add the asparagus to the boiling liquid, cover and cook for about 20 minutes over a low heat. Remove the pieces of asparagus.
4. Melt the butter in a saucepan, stir in the flour, then gradually add the asparagus liquid, stirring continuously.
5. Cook, stirring, until soup comes to the boil and thickens. Replace pieces of asparagus and gently mix in the cream. Reheat briefly and sprinkle with chopped parsley.
(Photo bottom)

Preparation time: 40 mins
Serves 2
Approx 130 kcal/540 kJ

Cream of Celeriac Soup

Ingredients Metric/Imperial

Celeriac	250 g/9 oz
Vegetable stock	450 ml/¾ pt
Single cream	30 ml/2 tbsp
Chopped fresh parsley	20 ml/4 tsp

1. Peel and dice the cerleriac. Put into a saucepan with the stock.
2. Cover and cook for about 10 minutes until tender.
3. Purée the soup, return to the pan and mix in the cream. Reheat briefly and garnish each portion with a sprinkling of parsley. *(Photo centre)*

Preparation time: 25 mins
Serves 1-2
Approx. 210 kcal/895 kJ

Cream of Celeriac Soup

Ingredients Metric/Imperial

Celeriac	250 g/9 oz
Vegetable stock	450 ml/¾ pt
Single cream	30 ml/2 tbsp
Chopped fresh parsley	20 ml/4 tsp

1. Peel and dice the cerleriac. Put into a saucepan with the stock.
2. Cover and cook for about 10 minutes until tender.
3. Purée the soup, return to the pan and mix in the cream. Reheat briefly and garnish each portion with a sprinkling of parsley.
(Photo centre)

Preparation time: 25 mins
Serves 1-2
Approx. 210 kcal/895 kJ

Pepper and Cabbage Soup

Ingredients	Metric/Imperial
Red pepper	1
Onion	1
Cold pressed sunflower oil	10 ml/2 tsp
Tomatoes	5
Vegetable stock powder	10 ml/2 tsp
Paprika	5 ml/1 tsp
Sauerkraut	100 g/4 oz
Single cream	20 ml/4 tsp
Chopped fresh parsley or chives	20 ml/4 tsp

1. Halve the pepper, remove the inside fibres and seeds and cut the flesh into strips.
2. Peel the onion and cut into rings. Gently fry the pepper strips with the onion rings in the oil in a saucepan for about 5 minutes.
3. Meanwhile, quarter the tomatoes. Purée the flesh then pass through a sieve for smoothness.
4. Season the tomato purée with instant stock powder and paprika. Stir into the vegetables.
5. Chop the sauerkraut and add to the soup. Cover and simmer for 10 minutes over a low heat. If necessary, add water to prevent the soup from becoming too thick.
6. Add the cream and sprinkle each portion with parsley or chives.
(Photo top)

Preparation time: 40 mins
Serves 2
Approx. 240 kcal/1005 kJ

Country Tomato Soup

Ingredients	Metric/Imperial
Celeriac	125 g/4½ oz
Large carrot	1
Small onion	1
Cold pressed olive oil	10 ml/2 tsp
Ripe tomatoes	6
Vegetable stock powder	10 ml/2 tsp
Italian seasoning	5 ml/1 tsp
Pinch of cayenne pepper	
Whipping cream	30 ml/2 tbsp
Sprig of fresh basil	1

1. Peel and dice the celeriac, carrot and onion, then fry gently in the oil in a saucepan until soft but still pale.
2. Blanch, skin and peel tomatoes then work to a purée. Rub through a sieve to remove the seeds.
3. Add the puréed tomato to the diced vegetables, cover and simmer over a low heat for about 12 minutes. Add water if necessary.
4. Purée the soup, return to the saucepan and reheat briefly. Garnish each serving with basil.
(Photo bottom)

Preparation time: 45 mins
Serves 2
Approx. 165 kcal/695 kJ

Carbohydrate-rich Main Meals

The colourful variety of the recipes in this chapter is a taster of what can be. Here you will find delicious potato, pasta and rice dishes, attractive savoury cakes, rich salads and sweet main dishes.

Try out something new, or look for ideas of how to revitalise old traditional recipes. The Combining Plan on pages 14 and 15 show which foods can be used to prepare a carbohydrate-rich meal. In addition, you can add as many of the neutral foods as you wish.

It is not always necessary to have meat on the table. With vegetables, pasta, rice and other cereals it is still possible to make memorable meals for the family. You will also find a number of rich salads that are easy to prepare and useful for packed lunches. Even a working person can enjoy healthy and varied food.

Potato Soup with Peas and Caraway

Ingredients	Metric/Imperial
Potatoes, peeled	300 g/11 oz
Vegetable stock	300 ml/½ pt
Large leek	1
Butter	20 ml/4 tsp
Carrots	3
Fresh or frozen peas	150 g/5 oz
Pinch of cayenne pepper	
Pinch of grated nutmeg	
Herb salt to taste	5 ml/1 tsp
Caraway seeds	30 ml/2 tbsp
Single cream	20 ml/ 4 tsp
Chopped fresh parsley	

1. Dice the potatoes and cook for about 18 minutes in the stock.
2. Meanwhile, clean the leek and cut into fine rings. Fry gently for a short time in the butter in a saucepan.
3. Peel the carrots, dice and combine with the peas. Stir into the leeks.
4. Remove half the diced potatoes from the stock and add to the pan of vegetables. Cover and simmer, stirring from time to time, for about 10 minutes.
5. Season the soup with cayenne pepper, nutmeg, herb salt and caraway.
6. Purée the remaining potatoes and stock and add to the fried vegetables. Stir in cream and sprinkle each portion with parsley.
(Photo bottom)

Preparation time: 50 mins
Serves 2
Approx. 360 kcal/1510 kJ

Potato and Leek Soup

Ingredients	Metric/Imperial
Potatoes, peeled	300 g/11 oz
Large leeks	2
Onion	1
Butter	10 ml/2 tsp
Water	600 ml/1 pt
Single cream	50 ml/2 fl oz
Vegetable stock powder	10 ml/2 tsp
Pinch of grated nutmeg	

1. Dice the potatoes finely. Clean the leek and cut into thin rings.
2. Peel the onion, chop finely and fry gently in the butter in a saucepan for about 5 minutes. Add the potatoes, the leeks and water and bring to the boil. Lower the heat and cover. Simmer over a lowish heat for 20 minutes.
3. Purée soup and return to the pan. Stir in the cream, stock powder and nutmeg. Reheat briefly and sprinkle with nutmeg before serving.
(Photo top)

Preparation time: 35 mins
Serves 2
Approx. 265 kcal/1105 kJ

Courgette and Potato Soup

Ingredients	Metric/Imperial
Courgettes	600 g/1 lb 6oz
Potatoes, peeled	300 g/11 oz
Vegetable stock powder	15 ml/1 tbsp
Water	300 ml/½ pt
Garlic clove, peeled and crushed	1
Single cream	50 g/2 fl oz

1. Cut the unpeeled courgettes and the potatoes into large pieces.
2. Put into a large saucepan with the stock powder and water. Bring to the boil, lower the heat and cover. Simmer for 15-18 minutes.
3. Add the garlic then work the soup to a fairly fine purée. Return to the saucepan, stir in the cream and reheat briefly before serving.
(Photo centre left)

Preparation time: 30 mins
Serves 2
Approx. 240 kcal/995 kJ

Note
If you wish to prepare the courgettes as a protein meal for two, cut about 600 g/1 lb 6 oz of cleaned courgettes into pieces and simmer in 600 ml/1 pt of water with about 15 ml/ 1 tbsp of vegetable stock powder for 10-12 minutes. Purée the vegetables and the liquid in which they were cooking, return to the saucepan and stand over a lower heat. Gradually whisk in 3 well beaten eggs and remove from heat.

Approx. 235 kcal/975 kJ

Carrot and Potato Stew

Ingredients Metric/Imperial

Carrots, peeled	600 g/1 lb 6 oz
Water	300 ml/½ pt
Potatoes, peeled	200 g/7 oz
Vegetable stock powder	10 ml/2 tsp
Glucose syrup	2.5 ml/½ tsp
Butter	10 ml/2 tsp
Chopped fresh parsley	30 ml/2 tbsp

1. Dice the carrots. Bring the water to the boil, add the diced carrots and cook in a covered saucepan on a low heat for about 5 minutes.
2. Meanwhile, dice the potatoes finely and add to the carrots. Simmer, covered for 12-15 minutes.
3. Add the next 3 ingredients and reheat briefly. Serve each portion sprinkled with parsley.
(Photo top)

Preparation time: 30 mins
Serves 2
Approx. 210 kcal/885 kJ

Spiced Potatoes with Tsatsiki

Ingredients	Metric/Imperial
For the potatoes:	
Potatoes	3
Cold pressed sunflower oil	30 ml/2 tbsp
Chopped mixed fresh herbs (marjoram, basil, sage)	30 ml/2 tbsp
Garlic clove, peeled and crushed	1
Paprika	5 ml/1 tsp
Herb salt	5 ml/1 tsp
For the tsatsiki:	
Thick Greek yoghurt	50 ml/¼ pt
Soy sauce	2.5 ml/½ tsp
Cold pressed olive oil	2.5 ml/½ tsp
Garlic clove, peeled and crushed	1
Cucumber, peeled and grated	75 g/3 oz
Sea salt to taste	
Chopped fresh dill	10 ml/2 tsp

1. Scrub the potatoes under cold running water, wipe dry and cut into 1 cm/½ in slices in their skins.
2. Mix the sunflower oil with the herbs and add the garlic, paprika and salt.
3. Pre-heat the oven to 200°C/400°F/gas mark 6. Brush both sides of the potato slices with the spiced oil and arrange on a baking tray. Bake for about 30-40 minutes or until golden brown, turning once or twice.
4. Meanwhile, prepare the tsatsiki. Place the yoghurt, soy sauce and olive oil in a bowl and beat with a whisk until smooth.
5. Add the garlic with the peeled and grated cucumber.
6. Stir both into the yoghurt and season with salt. Eat the baked potatoes with the tsatsiki, garnished with dill.
(Photo bottom)

Preparation time: 15 mins
Cooking time: 45 mins
Serves 1
Approx. 550 kcal/1880 kJ

Tip
Tsatsiki tastes good on wholemeal bread. One portion of tsatsiki contains 130 kcal/550 kJ.

Spinach Gratin

Ingredients Metric/Imperial

Waxy potatoes, all the same size	200 g/7 oz
Spinach	500 g/1 lb 2 oz
Butter for greasing	50 g/2 oz
Single cream	120 ml/4 fl oz
Water	60 g/2½ oz
Cheese (60% fat), (Gouda or Camembert)	1
Pinch of cayenne pepper	
Chopped fresh lovage	2.5 ml/½ tsp
Chopped fresh marjoram	2.5 ml/½ tsp
Vegetable stock powder	5 ml/1 tsp

1. Boil the potatoes in their skins for 12-15 minutes.
2. Meanwhile, blanch the spinach quickly in boiling water, then leave to drain.
3. Cool off the potatoes, then peel and cut into slices of equal thickness.
4. Arrange the spinach in a buttered soufflé dish and lay the potatoes on top like tiles.
5. Pre-heat the oven to 160°C/325°F/gas mark 3. Mix together the cream and water. Dice the cheese and add it to the mixture.
6. Season the mixture with the remaining ingredients and pour over the potato slices.
7. Place the gratin in the oven and bake for about 30 minutes until a warm golden brown.
(Photo opposite centre)

Preparation time: 35 mins
Cooking time: 30 mins
Serves 1
Approx. 615 kcal/2550 kJ

Grilled Potatoes with Dip

Ingredients Metric/Imperial

Wheat grains	40 g/1½ oz

For the potatoes:

Potatoes	4
Cold pressed sunflower oil	20 ml/4 tsp
Caraway seeds	10 ml/2 tsp
Chopped fresh marjoram	5 ml/1 tsp
Chopped fresh lovage	5 ml/1 tsp

For the dip:

Cucumber	1
Avocado	1
Spring onion	1
Thick Greek yoghurt	375 ml/13 fl oz
Herb salt to taste	
Garlic cloves, peeled and crushed	2

In addition:

Small dill sprigs	8

1. Cover the wheat grains with water and leave to soak overnight for about 8 hours.
2. Cook in the water in which it has soaked for about 25 minutes over a low heat, keeping the pan half covered.
3. Meanwhile, scrub the potatoes under cold running water until clean. Transfer to a saucepan, add a little water and par-boil for about 8 minutes.

Drain, cool to lukewarm and cut each in half lengthways.
4. Brush oil on to the cut surfaces and season with

caraway seeds, marjoram and lovage. Pre-heat the grill.
5. Place the halves together again and wrap each one in a double thickness of kitchen foil (matt side outwards). Grill the potatoes for 45-55 minutes, turning frequently and keeping the heat high.
6. Prepare the dip. Peel and finely dice the cucumber.
7. Peel the avocado, remove the centre stone and cut the flesh into small pieces. Trim the spring onion and cut into very thin rings.
8. Beat the yoghurt until smooth then add the prepared vegetables and the cooked wheat. Season with herb salt and add the crushed garlic.
9. Undo the foil around the potatoes, open out along the cuts and pack with dip. Garnish with dill.
(Photo bottom)

Preparation time: 30 mins plus soaking.
Cooking time: 55 mins
Serves 2
Approx. 750 kcal/3145 kJ

Jacket Potatoes with Quark

Ingredients Metric/Imperial

New potatoes	400 g/14 oz
Quark (20% fat)	250 g/9 oz
Mineral water	30 ml/2 tbsp
Bunch of chives	1
Sea salt	2.5 ml/½ tsp
Paprika	2.5 ml/½ tsp
Cucumber	1

1. Wash the potatoes and boil in their skins for 18-20 minutes.
2. Mix the quark with the mineral water, gently whisking until it looks creamy.
3. Finely chop the chives and add to the quark with the salt. Mix well and mix in the paprika.
4. Peel the cucumber and cut into 1 cm/½ in slices. Serve with the boiled potatoes and the quark mixture.
(Photo opposite top)

Preparation time: 30 mins
Serves 2
Approx. 300 kcal/1260 kJ

Mashed Potato with Sauerkraut and Fried Onion

Ingredients   Metric/Imperial

Potatoes	400 g/14 oz
Water	375 ml/13 fl oz
Sea salt to taste	
Vegetable stock powder	10 ml/2 tsp
Single cream	45 ml/3 tbsp
Sauerkraut	500 g/1 lb 2 oz
Large Spanish onion	1
Butter	15 ml/1 tbsp

1. Peel the potatoes and cut into small dice. Cook for about 15 minutes in boiling, salted water until soft. Keep the pan covered.
2. Mash the potatoes in their own cooking water then season with stock powder. Add the cream.
3. Chop the sauerkraut and warm in a saucepan over a moderate heat.
4. Peel the onion and cut into thin slices then separate into rings.
5. Heat the butter in a frying pan, add the onion rings and fry until golden, stirring frequently.
6. Mix the warm sauerkraut with the mashed potato, arrange on a warm plate and serve with the onion rings on top.
(Photo opposite top)

Preparation time: 35 mins
Serves 2
Approx. 570 kcal/2380 kJ

Fried Potatoes with Brussels Sprouts

Ingredients   Metric/Imperial

Cold, boiled potatoes	400 g/14 oz
Onion	1
Cold pressed sunflower oil	20 ml/4 tsp
Herb salt	5 ml/1 tsp
Brussels sprouts	500 g/1 lb 2 oz
Vegetable stock powder	5 ml/1 tsp
Pinch of grated nutmeg	1
Butter	15 ml/1 tbsp

1. Peel and slice the potatoes. Peel the onion, chop finely and fry lightly in the oil.
2. Add the potato slices, season with herb salt and fry fairly gently until they turn golden yellow.
3. Place the Brussels sprouts in a little water in a saucepan and season with the stock and the nutmeg. Cover.
4. Simmer for 8-12 minutes then transfer to a warm dish with the fried potatoes.
5. Brown the butter gently in a frying pan and pour over the vegetables. Serve fairly hot.
(Photo opposite centre)

Preparation time: 30 mins
Serves 2
Approx. 395 kcal/1645 kJ

Herrings in Cream with Potatoes

Ingredients   Metric/Imperial

For the herrings:

Salted herrings, 2 heads removed and filleted	
Soured cream	120 ml/4 fl oz
Thick yoghurt	175 ml/6 fl oz
Water	90 ml/6 tbsp
Onion	1
Soft apples	2
Juniper berries	5
Soy sauce	10 ml/2 tsp
Chopped fresh dill	20 ml/4 tsp

In addition:

Potatoes, boiled in skins	400 g/14 oz

Cut off the herring tails

Cut along the backbone

Remove the bones

1. Wash the salted herrings under cold running water. Cut off the tails and along the backbone with a sharp knife. Carefully remove the main bones from each and as many little bones as you can find.
2. Beat the soured cream and yoghurt with the water until creamy.
3. Peel the onion and cut into thin slices, then separate into rings. Quarter the apples then peel and core and cut into slender segments.
4. Add the onion and apple to the cream sauce with the juniper berries. Add the soy sauce and dill. Mix well and pour into a dish.
5. Add the herring fillets to the yoghurt sauce in a single layer then cover and refrigerate for about 24 hours. Serve with boiled potatoes.
(Photo opposite bottom)

Preparation time: 30 mins
Marinating time: 24 hrs
Serves 2
Approx. 625 kcal/2610 kJ

Note
Eat before a neutral salad, see pages 48-52.

Potato Salad with Herrings

Ingredients Metric/Imperial

Waxy potatoes	400 g/14 oz
Vegetable stock, hot	150 ml/¼ pt
Radishes	12
Spring onions	6
Small red pepper	1
Tomatoes	2

For the sauce:

Thick yoghurt	200 ml/7 fl oz
Soy sauce	10 ml/2 tsp
Cold pressed sunflower oil	10 ml/2 tsp
Herb salt to taste	
Bunches of fresh chives	2
Chopped fresh dill	30 ml/2 tbsp

In addition:

Small salted herring fillets	4

For the garnish:

Parsley sprigs	2
Red onion, sliced	1

1. Boil the potatoes in their skins, preferably on the previous day, and leave to cool. Peel and slice, put into a bowl and add the hot stock.

2. Cut the radishes and spring onions into thin rings.

3. Halve the pepper then remove the inside fibres and seeds. Cut the flesh into thin strips. Cut the tomatoes into segments. Place all the prepared vegetables into a bowl.

4. For the sauce, beat the yoghurt with the soy sauce, sunflower oil and herb salt.

5. Chop the chives and dill. Add to the yoghurt mixture, then toss with the prepared vegetables. Arrange on a dish and top with herring fillets, parsley and red onion slices.

Cooking time for potatoes: 30 mins
Preparation time: 35 mins
Approx. 690 kcal/2895 kJ

German Herring Salad

Ingredients Metric/Imperial

For the salad:

Small cooked beetroot	1
Medium potatoes	4
Onion	1
Soft apple	1
Walnuts	8
Salted herring fillets	4

For the sauce:

Soured cream	120 ml/5 fl oz
Thick yoghurt	100 ml/4 fl oz
Cold pressed sunflower oil	10 ml/2 tsp
Soy sauce	10 ml/2 tsp
Glucose syrup	10 ml/2 tsp

In addition:

Chopped fresh parsley	20 ml/4 tsp

1. Peel the beetroot and cut into small dice. Wash and scrub the potatoes and cook in their skins in boiling salted water for 20-25 minutes. Drain, cool and dice.

2. Peel the onion and chop finely. Peel and quarter the apple, remove the core and cut the flesh into narrow segments.

3. Chop the nuts coarsely. Cut the herring fillets into thin strips. Combine all the ingredients together in a bowl.

4. Mix the soured cream, yoghurt, oil, soy sauce and syrup well together. Toss with the herring mixture. Cover and leave in the refrigerator for 2 hours to marinate. Serve each portion sprinkled with parsley.

Preparation time: 1 hr
Marinating time: 3 hrs
Serves 2
Approx. 850 kcal/3545 kJ

Tip

If the salted herrings are very salty, lay them for a short time in water. To fillet the herrings yourself see page 72.

Mixed Vegetable Salad

Ingredients Metric/Imperial

Potatoes	2
Carrots	2
Green beans	150 g/5 oz
Vegetable stock	300 ml/½ pt
Tomatoes	2
Cucumber	½
Frozen sweet corn, thawed	100 g/4 oz

For the dressing:

Soured cream	120 ml/4 fl oz
Soy sauce	10 ml/2 tsp
Cold pressed sunflower oil	10 ml/2 tsp

In addition:

Feta cheese	125 g/4½ oz

1. Peel the potatoes and carrots and chop finely. String the beans and cut into pieces 4 cm/1½ in long.

2. Transfer the vegetables to a saucepan, add the vegetable stock and bring to the boil. Cover, lower the heat and simmer for about 15-18 minutes.

3. Remove the vegetables from the stock and leave to cool.

4. Dice the tomatoes.

5. Peel the cucumber and dice.

6. Combine all the vegetables, including defrosted corn, in a large bowl.

7. Make dressing by beating together the soured cream, soy sauce, oil and a little extra vegetable stock. Add the vegetables, toss well and crumble the feta cheese over the top.
(Photo bottom)

Preparation time: 35 mins
Serves 2
Approx. 385 kcal/1610 kJ

Vegetable Soup with Cheese Dumplings

Ingredients Metric/Imperial

For the soup:

Mixed vegetables made up of: carrots, kohlrabi, celeriac, cauliflower and green beans	800 g/1¾ lb
Onion	1
Butter	15 ml/1 tbsp
Vegetable stock	450 ml/¾ pt

For the dumplings

Day old wholemeal bread	75 g/3 oz
Hot water	100ml/3½floz
Single cream	30 ml/2 tbsp
Onion	1
Butter	5 ml/1 tsp
Chopped fresh parsley	15 ml/1 tbsp
Chopped fresh chives or basil	5 ml/1 tsp
Egg yolk	1
Sunflower seeds	15 ml/1 tbsp
Vegetable stock powder	8 ml/1½ tsp
Boiling salted water	750 ml/1¼ pts
Cheddar cheese	50 g/2 oz
Sea salt to taste	
Cornflour	30 ml/2 tbsp
Cold water	30 ml/2 tbsp

In addition:

Grated nutmeg to taste	
Chopped fresh parsley	15 ml/1 tbsp

1. Cut the carrots into pieces about 4 cm/1½ in thick. Cut the kohlrabi and the celeriac into strips and then divide the cauliflower into florets.

2. Cut the beans into lengths of about 2 cm/¾ in. Peel the onion, finely chop and fry lightly in the butter. Add all the other vegetables.

3. Add the stock, cover and leave the soup to simmer for 15-18 minutes.

4. Cut the bread into cubes, pour over hot water, add the cream and leave to soak for 3 minutes.

5. Peel the onion, chop finely and fry lighly in butter in a pan. Add to the bread with the parsley and chives or basil.

6. Work in the egg yolk, the sunflower seeds and the stock powder and mix well. Bring the salted water to the boil.

7. Dice the cheese. Form up dumplings from the bread mixture with damp hands and fill with the diced cheese and a sprinkling of salt.

8. Mix the cornflour with the cold water and add to the boiling stock. Add the dumplings and simmer, uncovered, for 8-10 minutes over a very low heat.

9. Season the soup with nutmeg, transfer to soup bowls and add the dumplings. Sprinkle each portion with parsley.
(Photo top)

Preparation time: 1¼ hrs
Serves 2
Approx. 405 kcal/1705 kJ

Spaghetti with Spicy Tomato Sauce

Ingredients Metric/Imperial

For the sauce:

Ripe tomatoes	400 g/14 oz
Red pepper	1
Pitted black olives	10
Cold pressed olive oil	10 ml/2 tsp
Cayenne pepper	2.5 ml/½ tsp
Chilli powder	2.5 ml/½ tsp
Rosemary	2.5 ml/½ tsp
Paprika	5 ml/1 tsp
Herb salt	5 ml/1 tsp
Garlic cloves, peeled and crushed	1-2
Chopped fresh parsley	30 ml/2 tbsp
Single cream	20 ml/4 tsp

In addiiton:

Wholemeal spaghetti	125 g/4½ oz
Boiling water	
Sea salt	

1. Blanch the tomatoes, remove the skins and coarsely chop the flesh.
2. Halve the pepper, remove the inside fibres and seeds, cut the flesh into squares and work to a purée with the tomatoes. Strain to remove the seeds.
3. Chop the olives. Work in the olive oil and next 5 ingredients.
4. Add the garlic then lastly mix in the chopped parsley and cream.
5. Cook the spaghetti in lightly salted water for 10-12 minutes until *al dente*. Drain and serve with the sauce.
(Photo centre)

Preparation time: 30 mins
Serves 2
Approx. 510 kcal/2145 kJ

Variation
You can opt for natural rice instead of noodles with the tomato sauce.

Pasta with Paprika and Mushroom Sauce

Ingredients Metric/Imperial

For the sauce:

Button mushrooms	350 g/12 oz
Butter	15 ml/1 tbsp
Large red pepper	1
Wholemeal flour	20 ml/4 tsp
Vegetable stock	300 ml/½ pt
Paprika	5 ml/1 tsp
Pinch of cayenne pepper	
Chopped fresh marjoram	2.5 ml/½ tsp
Herbes de Provence	5 ml/1 tsp
Single cream	30 ml/2 tbsp

In addition:

Wholemeal pasta	125 g/4½ oz
Water	
Sea salt	

1. Slice the mushrooms or leave whole and fry in the butter for about 3 minutes, turning. De-seed the pepper and cut the flesh into narrow strips.
2. Add the pepper to the mushrooms, sprinkle with the wholemeal flour and fry for about 2 minutes until absorbed. Cover with the stock and simmer for 5-8 minutes, stirring frequently.
3. Cook the pasta in lightly salted water for about 8-10 minutes until *al dente*.
4. Season the sauce with the spices and herbs then add the cream. Drain the pasta and coat with the sauce.
(Photo bottom)

Preparation time: 45 mins
Serves 2
Approx. 390 kcal/1645 kJ

Note
Eat with a neutral salad, see pages 48-52.

Spaghetti with Garlic Cream Sauce

Ingredients	Metric/Imperial
Wholemeal spaghetti	200 g/7 oz
Boiling water	5 ml/1 tsp
Sea salt	
Garlic cloves	2
Single cream	120 ml/4 fl oz
Herb salt	2.5 ml/½ tsp
Chopped fresh parsley or sage	20 ml/4 tsp

1. Cook the spaghetti in plenty of lightly salted water for about 8-10 minutes until *al dente*.
2. Peel the garlic and crush. Combine with the cream and season with herb salt.
3. Drain the spaghetti and mix with the seasoned cream sauce. Sprinkle with the parsley or sage. *(Photo top)*

Preparation time: 20 mins
Serves 2
Approx. 540 kcal/2265 kJ

Tip
This goes well with a tomato salad.

Tagliatelle with Vegetable Sauce

Ingredients Metric/Imperial

For the sauce:

Large onion	1
Carrots	2
Celeriac	75 g/3 oz
Single cream	100 ml/3½ fl oz
Water	400 ml/14 fl oz
Bay leaves	2
Pinch of grated nutmeg	
Sea salt	5 ml/1 tsp
Butter	30 ml/2 tbsp
Wholemeal flour	30 ml/2 tbsp
Red pepper	1
Frozen sweet corn, thawed	30 ml/2 tbsp

In addition:

Wholemeal tagliatelle or home-made spätzle (see tip)	125 g/4½ oz
Sea salt	
Boiling water	

1. Peel the onion, the carrots and celeriac and cut into small dice.
2. Put the cream and water into a saucepan, add the vegetables, bay leaves, nutmeg and sea salt and bring to the boil.
3. Simmer, covered, for about 5 minutes. Remove the saucepan from the heat and leave to stand for about 30 minutes.
4. Sieve the vegetable mixture into a bowl. Leave the vegetables on one side and remove the bay leaves.
5. Melt the butter in a small saucepan, stir in the flour and whisk for 1 minute until smooth.

Gradually add the vegetable water.
6. Bring the sauce to the boil, stirring all the time, and leave to simmer until it thickens, stirring almost constantly. Cook the tagliatelle or spätzle for 10-12 minutes in boiling salted water until *al dente*.
7. De-seed the pepper and dice the flesh finely. Add to the wholemeal flour sauce with the sweet corn and the cooked diced vegetables.
8. Drain the pasta and serve with the vegetable sauce.
(Photo opposite bottom)

Preparation time: 1¼ hrs
Serves 2
Approx. 620 kcal/2590 kJ

Tip
German, Swiss and Austrian noodles, called spätzle, are easy to make at home. For two portions you will need 2 egg yolks, 1 pinch of sea salt, 100 g/ 4 oz wholemeal flour and 5 ml/1 tsp vegetable stock powder. Whisk together the egg yolks, 100 ml/ 4 fl oz of water and a pinch of salt and then combine with the flour. Leave the dough to rest for about 30 minutes, keeping the bowl covered.

Spread the noodle dough on a wooden board.

Scrape the dough into the boiling water.

Bring 750 ml/1¼ pts of water to the boil and season with instant stock.
Spread out the noodle dough, a portion at a time, on a wooden board. Dip a palette knife into boiling water and then scrape off the dough, in fine strips, into the water. The finer they are the better. Leave the noodles to simmer for about 3 minutes, then lift them out with a ladle and rinse quickly with cold water.

Spaghetti on Vegetables

Ingredients Metric/Imperial

For the vegetables:

Small onion	1
Garlic clove	1
Cold pressed olive oil	10 ml/2 tsp
Mushrooms	100 g/4 oz
Aubergine	150 g/5 oz
Small red pepper	1
Small courgette	1
Oregano	5 ml/1 tsp
Rosemary	5 ml/1 tsp
Pinch of cayenne pepper	
Vegetable stock powder	5 ml/1 tsp
Single cream	20 ml/4 tsp
Chopped fresh basil	20 ml/4 tsp

In addition:

Wholemeal spaghetti	60 g/2½ oz
Sea salt	
Water	

1. Peel the onion and cut into thin slices. Peel the garlic and crush. Lightly fry both in the oil.
2. Slice the mushrooms finely. Clean and dice the aubergine, the pepper and courgette.
3. Add the mushrooms and the vegetables to the onion and fry gently for about 10 minutes, stirring frequently.
4. Cook the spaghetti in boiling salted water for 8-10 minutes until *al dente*.
5. Season the vegetables well with the oregano, rosemary, cayenne pepper and instant stock. Mix in the cream and transfer to a plate.
6. Drain the pasta and arrange on top of the vegetables. Sprinkle each portion with basil.
(Photo opposite top)

Preparation time: 1 hr
Serves 1
Approx. 470 kcal/1970 kJ

Macaroni Napoli

Ingredients	Metric/Imperial
For the sauce:	
Aubergine	300 g/11 oz
Onion	1
Garlic cloves	2
Red pepper	1
Cold pressed olive oil	20 ml/4 tsp
Rosemary	5 ml/1 tsp
Chilli powder	5 ml/1 tsp
Herbs de Provence	5 ml/1 tsp
Vegetable stock powder	5 ml/1 tsp
Ripe tomatoes	2
In addition:	
Wholemeal macaroni	100 g/4 oz
Sea salt	
A few basil leaves	

1. Pre-heat the oven to 220°C/425°F/gas mark 7. Remove the aubergine stalk. Wrap the whole aubergine in oiled foil, matt side outwards. Bake for about 40 minutes.
2. Peel and dice the onion. Peel and slice the garlic. De-seed pepper and chop the flesh fairly finely. Fry all these in the oil for about 3 minutes.
3. Season the vegetables with the rosemary, chilli, Provence herbs and instant stock. Remove from the heat.
4. Unwrap the cooked aubergine from the foil. remove the skin and chop the flesh finely. Add it to the vegetable mixture, then work to a purée. Leave to cool.

5. Blanch and skin the tomatoes, cut into quarters and rub through a sieve. Add to the cold vegetable mixture and add seasoning as required.
6. Cook the macaroni in lightly salted water for 8-10 minutes until *al dente*. Drain well and serve with the cold vegetable sauce. Garnish with a few basil leaves, cut into strips.

Preparation time: 1¼ hrs
Serves 2
Approx. 325 kcal/1355 kJ

Pasta Salad with Mushrooms

Ingredients	Metric/Imperial
Wholemeal pasta shapes	100 g/4 oz
Mushrooms	250 g/9 oz
Butter	15 ml/1 tbsp
Italian seasoning	5 ml/1 tsp
Vegetable stock powder	5 ml/1 tsp
Tomatoes	2
Yellow pepper	1

For the sauce:

Thick yoghurt	175 ml/6 fl oz
Soy sauce	10 ml/2 tsp
Garlic clove	1
Herb salt to taste	

In addition:

Pitted black olives	6
A few basil leaves	

1. Cook the pasta in lightly salted water for 10-12 minutes until *al dente*.
2. Meanwhile, slice the mushrooms finely. Melt the butter in a frying pan, and fry the mushrooms over a medium heat until the liquid produced has evaporated.
3. Season the mushrooms with the Italian seasoning and the stock powder and leave to cool. Drain the pasta and cool.
4. Dice the tomatoes. De-seed the pepper and cut the flesh into fine strips.
5. To make the salad sauce, combine the yoghurt with soy sauce. Peel and crush in the garlic clove then season with herb salt.
6. Toss the sauce with all prepared salad ingredients and the cold pasta. Garnish with olives and basil leaves.

Preparation time: 50 mins
Serves 2
Approx. 460 kcal/1915 kJ

Rice with Mixed Mushrooms

Ingredients   Metric/Imperial

Brown or white rice	100 g/4 oz
Mixed mushrooms	400 g/14 oz
Onion	1
Butter	15 ml/1 tbsp
Wholemeal flour	45 ml/3 tbsp
Vegetable stock	150 ml/¼ pt
Soured cream	20 ml/2 tbsp
Chopped fresh parsley or chervil	20 ml/4 tsp

1. Cover the rice with water and leave for 8 hours to soak (or overnight). Cook the rice over a low heat the next day for about 25 minutes.
2. Clean the mushrooms and chop finely. Peel the onion and dice finely.
3. Melt the butter in a frying pan, add the onion and fry until pale gold.
4. Add the mushrooms and sprinkle with wholemeal flour. Gradually pour on the vegetable stock and bring to the boil, stirring all the time. Cover and simmer for 15-20 minutes, stirring frequently.
5. Mix in the cream and serve with the rice. Sprinkle the parsley or chervil over each portion to garnish.
(Photo opposite top)

Soaking time: 8 hrs
Preparation time: 45 mins
Serves 2
Approx. 160 kcal/665 kJ

Vegetable and Mushroom Fry

Ingredients   Metric/Imperial

Small carrots	3
Courgette	1
Oyster mushrooms	125 g/4½ oz
Mangetout	100 g/4 oz
Butter	10 ml/2 tsp
Vegetable stock powder	8 ml/1½ tsp
Curry powder	5 ml/1 tsp
Single cream	45 ml/3 tbsp
Cold water	90 ml/6 tbsp
Egg yolk	1
Millet	20 ml/4 tsp
Chopped, mixed fresh herbs (parsley, lovage, marjoram)	30 ml/2 tbsp

1. Peel the carrots and thinly slice. Top and tail the courgette. Clean the oyster mushrooms if necessary.
2. Slice the courgette and cut the mushrooms coarsely. Clean the mangetout.
3. Melt the butter in a frying pan, add the carrot slices and fry for about 4 minutes over a medium heat. Add the prepared vegetables and continue to fry gently for 8-10 minutes.
4. Season with the stock powder and the curry. Whisk the cream with the water, egg yolk and millet. Stir into the vegetables, bring to the boil, simmer briefly until thickened and sprinkle each portion with the herbs.
(Photo opposite centre)

Preparation time: 40 mins
Serves 1
Approx. 535 kcal/2250 kJ

Mushroom Risotto

Ingredients   Metric/Imperial

Onion	1
Leek	1
Butter	15 ml/1 tbsp
Mushrooms	350 g/12 oz
Vegetable stock	450 ml/¾ pt
Millet	100 g/4 oz
Pinch of grated nutmeg	
Soured cream	20 ml/4 tsp
Chopped fresh parsley	20 ml/4 tsp

1. Peel the onion, clean the leek and cut both into small pieces.
2. Fry gently in the butter for 3-4 minutes. Meanwhile, clean the mushrooms, halve the larger ones and add to the onion and leek. Fry for 5 minutes. then pour in the vegetable stock.
3. Rinse the millet in hot water, add to the pan of mushrooms and cover. Simmer for 25-30 minutes, stirring from time to time.
4. Season with nutmeg. Stir in the soured cream and sprinkle each portion with the parsley.
(Photo opposite bottom)

Preparation time: 1 hr
Serves 2
Approx. 320 kcal/1345 kJ

Note
Eat a small, neutral salad with this dish (see pages 48-52).

Mushrooms au Gratin

Ingredients	Metric/Imperial
Large mushrooms	8
Herb salt	5 ml/1 tsp
Millet	75 g/3 oz
Onion	1
Butter	20 ml/4 tsp
Garlic cloves, peeled and crushed	2
Hot water	450 ml/¾ pt
Leaf spinach	600 g/1½ lb
Pine kernels or chopped almonds	45 ml/3 tbsp
Vegetable stock powder	10 ml/2 tsp
Single cream	45 ml/3 tbsp
Cheddar cheese	150 g/5 oz

1. Clean the mushrooms, twist out the stalks and chop finely. Leave the heads whole, season with a little herb salt and put to one side.
2. Rinse the millet in hot water. Peel the onion and dice finely. Fry both for about 5 minutes in the butter. Add the chopped mushroom stalks and the garlic.
3. Fry gently for 5-8 minutes. Add the water and leave to simmer, covered, for 20-25 minutes until the millet has swollen and is soft.
4. Clean the spinach, blanch quickly in boiling water, leave to drain and then tear into large pieces.
5. Add the spinach and the pine kernels or almonds to the millet and season with the stock powder. Mix in the cream.
6. Pre-heat the oven to 200°C/400°F/gas mark 6. Fill the mushroom heads with part of the millet and spinach mixture. Spoon the rest into a soufflé dish and place the stuffed mushroom heads on top.
7. Thinly slice the cheese, arrange on top of the mushrooms and bake for 10-15 minutes or until the cheese is brown and the mushrooms are hot.
(Photo opposite top)

Preparation time: 45 mins
Cooking time: 10-15 mins
Serves 2
Approx. 775 kcal/3235 kJ

Mixed Vegetables with Rice

Ingredients	Metric/Imperial
Brown rice	100 g/4 oz
Salsify	300 g/11 oz
Dash of vinegar	
Carrots	2
Butter	20 ml/4 tsp
Button mushrooms	150 g/5 oz
Fresh or frozen peas, thawed	150 g/5 oz
Vegetable stock	300 ml/½ pt
Arrowroot	15 ml/1 tbsp
Single cream	50 g/2 oz
Egg yolk	1
Chopped fresh parsley	30 ml/2 tbsp

1. Cover the rice with water and soak for 8 hours.
2. Cook the rice over a low heat in a covered saucepan for about 25 minutes.
3. Peel the salsify thinly or scrape, but wear plastic gloves as juices from the vegetable can leave dark spots on the skin. Cut the salsify in pieces and drop immediately into vinegar water (mix 450 ml/¾ pt water with a good dash of vinegar), to prevent browning.
4. Peel the carrots, slice thinly and fry in butter for 3-4 minutes. Add the mushrooms, peas and salsify.
5. Add the vegetable stock, cover the pan and simmer for 15-20 minutes.
6. Mix the arrowroot smoothly with a little cold water. Add to the vegetables, bring to the boil and simmer, stirring, until thickened.
7. Whisk the cream with the egg yolk and add. Reheat without boiling. Serve the vegetables on top of the rice and sprinkle with parsley.
(Photo opposite bottom)

Soaking time: 8 hrs
Preparation time: 1¼ hrs
Serves 2
Approx. 525 kcal/2205 kJ

Tip
In order to protect one's hands, the cleaned, but unpeeled salsify can be cooked for about 20 minutes in vinegar water. It is then easy to pull off the skin.

Rice Salad

Ingredients	Metric/Imperial
Brown rice	100 g/4 oz
Yellow pepper	1
Cucumber	½
Tomatoes	3
Button mushrooms	125 g/4½ oz
Sunflower seeds	20 ml/4 tsp

For the sauce:

Thick yoghurt	175 ml/6 fl oz
Soy sauce	10 ml/2 tsp
Glucose syrup	5 ml/1 tsp
Herb salt	5 ml/1 tsp
Chopped fresh herbs (dill, basil, parsley)	30 ml/2 tbsp

In addition:

Soy bean sprouts (home-grown, see page 21, or bought)	30 ml/2 tbsp

1. Cover the rice with water and leave to soak for 8 hours.
2. Cook over a low heat in a covered saucepan for about 25 minutes. Tip into a sieve, rinse with cold water and leave to drain thoroughly.
3. De-seed the pepper and cut the flesh into strips.
4. Peel the cucumber and cut into pieces of about 1 cm/½ in.
5. Cut each tomato into 8 pieces. Slice the mushrooms thinly.

6. Mix the prepared vegetables with the rice and the sunflower seeds.
7. Stir the yoghurt with the soy sauce, glucose syrup and herb salt.
8. Mix in the herbs and add the sauce to the salad ingredients. Toss thoroughly and sprinkle with soy bean sprouts.
(Photo top) bottom

Soaking time: 8 hrs
Preparation time: 50 mins
Serves 2
Approx. 390 kcal/1635 kJ

Vegetable Pilau

Ingredients	Metric/Imperial
Brown rice	100 g/4 oz
Onion	1
Butter	15 ml/1 tbsp
Vegetable stock	400 ml/14 fl oz
Frozen sweet corn, thawed	200 g/7 oz
Fresh or frozen peas, thawed	200 g/7 oz
Pinch of saffron	
Single cream	100 ml/3½ fl oz
Chopped fresh parsley	20 ml/4 tsp
Flaked almonds	20 ml/4 tsp

1. Cover the rice with water and leave to soak for 8 hours.
2. Rinse well and leave to drain thorugh a sieve.
3. Peel the onion, dice finely and fry in the butter for about 4 minutes. Add the drained rice with the vegetable stock, cover and leave to simmer for about 20 minutes.
4. Add the sweet corn and the peas. Continue to simmer for another 5 minutes, stirring frequently.
5. Mix in the saffron then fork in the cream and parsley. Sprinkle each portion with almond flakes.
(Photo opposite top)

Soaking time: 8 hrs
Preparation time: 45 mins
Serves 2
Approx. 630 kcal/2640 kJ

Note
Accompany with a small neutral salad (see pages 48-52).

Carbohydrate-rich Main Meals

Oat Flake Burgers with Garlic

Ingredients Metric/Imperial

For the burgers:

Rolled oats	75g /3 oz
Onion	1
Butter	5 ml/1 tsp
Vegetable stock	150 ml/¼ pt
Pinch of celery salt	
Paprika	5 ml/1 tsp
Chopped fresh parsley	15 ml/1 tbsp
Gorgonzola	30 g/1½ oz
Wholemeal breadcrumbs	10 ml/2 tsp
Cold pressed sunflower oil	15 ml/1 tbsp

For the sauce:

Thick yoghurt	60 g/2½ oz
Garlic clove, peeled and crushed	1
Pinch of herb salt	

1. Lightly crush the rolled oats in a brown paper bag.
2. Peel the onion, chop finely and fry in the butter until soft.
3. Add the oat flakes and the vegetable stock. Stir well and simmer until the mixture thickens. Cool to lukewarm.
4. Stir in the celery salt, paprika and parsley. Knead well and leave to stand for 10 minutes.
5. Prepare the garlic sauce. Whisk the yoghurt until smooth then crush in the peeled garlic and season with herb salt.
6. Form the oat mixture into 4 rounds with damp hands. Sandwich together with the gorgonzola and pinch the edges together to seal.
8. Toss in bread crumbs and fry in the oil until crispy, turning twice.
(Photo opposite bottom)

Preparation time: 30 mins
Serves 1-2
Approx. 410 kcal/1715 kJ

Vegetable Paella

Ingredients Metric/Imperial

Brown rice	100 g/4 oz
Red peppers	2
Mushrooms	225 g/8 oz
Onions	2
Cold pressed olive oil	10 ml/2 tsp
Leeks	2
Frozen peas, thawed	45 ml/3 tbsp
Garlic cloves, peeled and crushed	2
Vegetable stock powder	10 ml/2 tsp
Hot water	300 ml/½ pt
Saffron powder	2.5 ml/½ tsp
Thick yoghurt	30 ml/2 tbsp
Chopped fresh parsley	20 ml/4 tsp

1. Cover the rice with water and leave to soak for about 8 hours.
2. Cook in a closed saucepan over a low heat for about 30 minutes.
3. Meanwhile, de-seed the peppers and cut flesh into strips. Thinly slice the mushrooms.
4. Peel and chop the onions and fry in the oil until soft. Clean the leeks, cut into rings and add to the onions.
5. Mix in the pepper strips, peas, garlic and mushrooms.
6. Add the vegetable stock powder and the water and cook for about 15 minutes.
7. Mix the rice with the vegetables and leave to stand for about 5 minutes.
8. Stir in the saffron and yoghurt and sprinkle each serving with parsley.
(Photo opposite top)

Soaking time: 8 hrs
Preparation time: 45 mins
Serves 2
Approx. 450 kcal/1980 kJ

Potatao Cheese Gratin

Ingredients Metric/Imperial

Potatoes	400 g/14 oz
Water	200 ml/7 fl oz
Single cream	45 ml/3 tbsp
Gorgonzola or Camembert (60% fat)	75 g/3 oz
Vegetable stock powder	10 ml/2 tsp
Pinch of cayenne pepper	
Chopped fresh marjoram leaves	5 ml/1 tsp

1. Wash the potatoes and cook for about 15 minutes in boiling, salted water in their skins. Drain, leave until cool, then peel and cut into slices of equal thickness.
2. Arrange like roof tiles in a short gratin dish (see picture). Pre-heat the oven to 160°C/325°F/gas mark 3.
3. Mix the water with the cream. Cut the cheese into small dice then add to the mixture.
4. Season with the vegetable stock and cayenne pepper and pour over the potatoes.
5. Sprinkle with marjoram and bake the gratin for 18-20 minutes until it turns golden brown and crusty.
(Photo opposite centre)

Preparation time: 1 hr
Serves 2
Approx. 405 kcal/1695 kJ

Note
Choose a neutral salad to eat with the gratin (see pages 48-52).

Pizza Romana

Ingredients   Metric/Imperial

For the dough:

Fresh yeast	25 g/1 oz
Warm water	130ml/4½floz
Wholemeal flour	200 g/7 oz
Five-spice powder	2.5 ml/½ tsp
Coriander	5 ml/1 tsp
Sea salt	2.5 ml/½ tsp
Cold pressed sunflower oil	5 ml/1 tsp
Butter for greasing	

For the filling:

Green pepper	1
Red pepper	1
Small fennel bulb	1
Small leek	1
Spanish onion	1
Cold pressed olive oil	10 ml/2 tsp
Herb salt	5 ml/1 tsp
Oregano or Italian seasoning	8 ml/1½ tsp
Garlic clove	1
Vegetable stock powder	5 ml/1 tsp
Mozzarella cheese	75 g/3 oz
Chopped mixed fresh herbs (marjoram, basil, thyme, parsley)	30 ml/2 tbsp

1. Dissolve the yeast in the warm water and mix with half the wholemeal flour to form a dough. Cover and leave to rise in a warm place for 20 minutes.

2. Add the rest of the flour, the five-spice powder, coriander, salt and sunflower oil then knead to a smooth and pliable dough.

3. Grease a pizza tray about 28 cm/11 in in diameter with butter. Press the dough evenly over the base and prick all over with a fork. Leave in a warm place to rise until it doubles its size; about 20 minutes.

4. Clean and de-seed the pepper and cut the flesh into thin strips. Wash the fennel, leek and onion and cut into fine strips or slices.

5. Fry all the vegetables in the olive oil for about 7 minutes, then season with herb salt and oregano or Italian seasoning. Peel and crush the garlic and add.

6. Pre-heat the oven to 200°C/400°F/gas mark 6. Spread the vegetables over the dough and sprinkle the stock powder on top.

7. Place the pizza in the oven and bake it for 15 minutes.

8. Cut the cheese into strips, mix with the herbs and spread over the pizza. Bake for a further 8 minutes until the cheese is golden yellow.

9. Cut the pizza into 8 pieces and accompany with a small neutral salad.

Preparation time: 1¼ hrs
Baking time: 15 mins
Serves 2
Approx. 620 kcal/2605 kJ

Onion Flan

Ingredients Metric/Imperial

For the dough:

Fresh yeast	25 g/1 oz
Water	130ml/4½floz
Wholemeal flour	200 g/7 oz
Sea salt	2.5 ml/½ tsp
Cold pressed sunflower oil	5 ml/1 tsp
Butter for greasing	

For the filling:

Spanish onions	1 kg/2 lb
Soft margarine	10 ml/2 tsp
Single cream	100ml/3½floz
Water	50 ml/2 oz
Egg yolks	2
Mozzarella cheese	75 g/3 oz
Grated nutmeg	2.5 ml/½ tsp
Pinch of cayenne pepper	
Herb salt	5 ml/1 tsp
Five-spice powder	5 ml/1 tsp
Coriander	5 ml/1 tsp

1. Dissolve the yeast in the warm water and stir in half the wholemeal flour. Cover and leave to rise for about 20 minutes in a warm place.

2. Add the rest of the flour, the sea salt and oil then knead to a smooth and pliable dough. Cover and leave to stand in a warm place until the dough has risen to twice its size, about 20 minutes.

3. Peel the onions and cut into thin slices. Heat the margarine in a frying pan, add the onions and fry gently until soft.

4. Mix the cream with the water and whisk in the egg yolks.

5. Cut the cheese into small dice and add to the cream and egg mixture. Season with nutmeg, cayenne pepper, herb salt, five-spice powder and coriander.

6. Pour the cream sauce on the onions and stir everything well together.

7. Pre-heat the oven to 180°C/350°F/gas mark 4. Knead the dough thoroughly again and press into a buttered baking tin measuring 26 cm/10 in in diameter, making sure it covers the sides.

8. Cover with the onion mixture and bake for about 35 minutes.

**Preparation time: 1 hr
Baking time: 35 mins
Approx. 480 kcal/2015 kJ**

Note
Eat a small neutral salad with the flan (see pages 48-52).

Tip
Onion flan is delicious eaten cold or warm between meals. It will serve 8 as a snack.

Pancake with Goat's Cheese Filling

Ingredients	Metric/Imperial
Wholemeal flour	500 g/1lb 2oz
Sea salt	10 ml/2 tsp
Water	300 ml/½ pt
Mild goat's cheese	250 g/9 oz
Cold pressed sunflower oil or olive oil	150 ml/¼ pt
Honey	45 ml/3 tbsp

1. Gradually add the flour and sea salt to the water and knead to a smooth and pliable dough. Leave to stand for about 15 minutes.
2. Divide the dough into 8 even-sized pieces and shape into balls. Cut the cheese into 8 pieces.
3. Press little hollows into the centre of each ball and insert cheese into each. Close up so that the cheese is buried inside each ball.
4. Flatten gently with your hand, making sure no cheese is visible.
5. Fry individually in the oil until golden brown, turning twice. Spread with honey and serve hot.
(Photo top)

Preparation time: 1½ hrs
Serves 4
Approx. 620 kcal/2605 kJ

Note
Eat with a neutral salad (see pages 48-52).

Mixed Pizza Bread

Ingredients	Metric/Imperial
Onion	1
Button mushrooms	100 g/4 oz
Yellow pepper	1
Cold pressed olive oil	10 ml/2 tsp
Oregano	5 ml/1 tsp
Herb salt	5 ml/1 tsp
Wholemeal bread	4 slices
Butter	10 ml/2 tsp
Cheddar cheese, grated	75 g/ 3 oz
Red peppers	3

1. Peel the onion and thinly slice. Finely slice the mushrooms.
2. De-seed the peppers and cut the flesh into narrow strips.
3. Fry the prepared vegetables in the oil for 6 minutes, then season with oregano and herb salt. Pre-heat the oven to 180°C/350°F/gas mark 4.
4. Spread the bread thinly with the butter and arrange the vegetables on top. Sprinkle with the cheese then bake for about 8 minutes. Alternatively, grill until golden.
5. De-seed the red peppers, cut into strips and eat with the bread.
(Photo centre)

Preparation time: 30 mins
Serves 2
Approx. 475 kcal/1980 kJ

Corn Dumplings with Sauerkraut

Ingredients	Metric/Imperial
For the dumplings:	
Onion	1
Butter	15 ml/1 tbsp
Cornmeal or polenta	150 g/5 oz
Water	300 ml/½ pt
Vegetable stock powder	30 ml/2 tbsp
Chopped fresh parsley or dill	5 ml/1 tsp
Garlic clove, peeled and crushed	1
Sunflower seeds	30 ml/2 tbsp
Egg yolk	1
For the sauerkraut:	
Small onion	1
Cold pressed sunflower oil	10 ml/2 tsp
White cabbage	600 g/1 lb 6 oz
Margarine	10 ml/2 tsp
Water	150 ml/¼ pt
Juniper berries	5
Five-spice powder	5 ml/1 tsp
Bay leaf	1
Water	800 ml/1¼ pts
In addition:	
Potato starch	30 ml/2 tbsp
Cold water	30 ml/2 tbsp

1. For dumplings, peel the onion then finely chop and fry gently in the butter until soft.

2. Sprinkle with the cornmeal, stir quickly together and add the water. Bring to the boil on a low heat, stirring continuously. Mix in the instant stock powder with the parsley, then add the garlic.

3. Add the sunflower seeds to the mixture with the egg yolk. Cook over a low heat, stirring continuously, until thickened. Remove the saucepan from the heat and leave for about 1 hour to give the dough time to mature.

4. Peel the onion, dice finely and fry in the oil until soft.

5. Chop the cabbage, add to the onion and lightly fry together for about 6 minutes.

6. Add the margarine to the cabbage and pour on the water. Add the juniper berries, five-spice powder and bay leaf. Cover and braise for 20 minutes.

7. Bring the water to the boil and lightly salt. Mix the potato starch with the cold water until smooth. Add to the boiling water. Boil until thickened.

8. Shape the cornmeal mixture into small dumplings with damp hands and cook, uncovered, in the pan of thickened water for about 10 minutes over a very low heat.

9. Before serving, remove the bay leaf from the sauerkraut and eat with the dumplings.
(Photo bottom)

**Preparation time: 1¾ hrs
Serves 2
Approx. 590 kcal/2470 kJ**

Wheaten Cauliflower and Mushrooms

Ingredients	Metric/Imperial
Wheat grains	40 g/1½ oz
Medium cauliflower	1
Sea salt to taste	
Button mushrooms	225 g/8 oz
Spring onions	4
Butter	10 ml/2 tsp
Vegetable stock	300 ml/½ pt
Soured cream	100ml/3½floz
Mild curry powder	10 ml/2 tsp
Chopped fresh parsley	30 ml/2 tbsp

1. Cover the wheat grains with water and leave to stand for 8 hours.
2. Cook for 25 minutes in salted water over a low heat in a closed saucepan.
3. Divide the cauliflower into florets. Cook in lightly salted water for 8-10 minutes.
4. Slice the mushrooms thinly and cut the spring onions into fine rings.
5. Melt the butter in a frying pan and lightly fry the mushrooms and onion.
6. Add the cauliflower florets and stir-fry for 3 minutes. Pour on the vegetable stock and simmer for about 5 minutes.
7. Mix in the cooked wheat grains. Mix the soured cream with the curry powder and stir into the vegetables. Sprinkle parsley over each portion. *(Photo opposite bottom)*

Soaking time: 8 hrs
Preparation time: 1 hr
Serves 2
Approx. 295 kcal/1245 kJ

Wheat Salad with Sheep's Cheese

Ingredients	Metric/Imperial
Wheat grains	100 g/4 oz
Sea salt	5 ml/1 tsp
Medium cucumber	1
Tomatoes	3
Spring onions	3
Pitted black olives	10
Frozen sweet corn, thawed	45 ml/3 tbsp

For the sauce:

Soy sauce	15 ml/1 tbsp
Water	100 ml/4 fl oz
Herb salt	5 ml/1 tsp
Cold pressed olive oil	10 ml/2 tsp

In addition:

Sheep's cheese	100 g/4 oz
Basil sprig	1
Chopped fresh parsley	45 ml/3 tbsp

1. Cover the wheat grains with water and leave to soak for 8 hours.
2. Cook the grains in salted water over a low heat in a closed saucepan for about 25 minutes. Leave to cool.
3. Peel the cucumber, halve lengthways and slice. Cut each tomato into 8 segments.
4. Clean the spring onions and cut into fine rings.
5. Mix the cucumber, tomatoes, spring onions and olives in a large bowl. Add the sweet corn and cooked grains.
6. To make the sauce, mix the soy sauce with the water and herb salt and then beat in the oil. Toss the sauce with the salad ingredients.
7. Dice the sheep's cheese and sprinkle evenly on top. Garnish with the basil and parsley. *(Photo opposite centre)*

Soaking time: 8 hrs
Preparation time: 45 mins
Serves 2
Approx. 625 kcal/2620 kJ

Rice Pudding

Ingredients	Metric/Imperial
Short-grain pudding rice	100 g/4 oz
Sea salt to taste	
Thick yoghurt	175 ml/6 fl oz
Clear honey	20 ml/4 tsp
Raisins	20 ml/4 tsp
Chopped almonds	20 ml/4 tsp
Cinnamon	5 ml/1 tsp

1. Cover the rice with water and leave to soak for about 8 hours.
2. Cook the rice in lightly salted water over a low heat in a covered saucepan for about 25 minutes. Leave to cool.
3. Mix the cooked rice with the yoghurt, honey and raisins. Sprinkle with cinnamon and almonds. *(Photo opposite top)*

Soaking time: 8 hrs
Preparation time: 35 mins
Serves 2
Approx. 375 kcal/1570 kJ

Note
Eat a neutral salad beforehand (see pages 48-52).

Semolina Dumplings with Apple Purée

Ingredients Metric/Imperial

For the dumplings:

Flaked almonds	40 g/1½ oz
Water	200 ml/7 fl oz
Single cream	30 ml/2 tbsp
Wholemeal semolina	125 g/4½ oz
Egg yolk	1
Clear honey	20 ml/4 tsp

In addition:

Sea salt	5 ml/1 tsp

For the purée:

Soft apples	450 g/1 lb
Water	150 ml/¼ pt
Small cinnamon stick	1
Clear honey	10 ml/2 tsp
Cinnamon	5 ml/1 tsp

1. Toast the almonds in a frying pan without oil until golden brown. Pour on the water and cream then bring to the boil.

2. Gradually trickle in the wholemeal semolina and cook over a low heat for about 5 minutes, until the semolina is firm enough to be shaped.

3. Leave the semolina to cool a little then stir in the egg yolk and honey.

4. Bring some lightly salted water to the boil. Using 2 teaspoons, cut out small dumplings from the semolina mixture and cook in the simmering water for about 5 minutes until they rise to the surface.

5. Prepare the purée. Peel, quarter and core the apples and cut the flesh into thin slices.

6. Cook the apples, water and cinnamon for about 10 minutes or until very soft, keeping the pan half covered. Remove the cinnamon stick.

7. Mash the apples finely then work to a purée with a whisk.

8. Leave the purée to cool a little and sweeten with the honey. Serve the semolina dumplings with the apple purée and sprinkle with cinnamon.

**Preparation time: 35 mins
Serves 2
Approx. 600 kcal/2520 kJ**

Almond Pancakes

Ingredients   Metric/Imperial

For the pancakes:
Wholemeal flour	50 g/2 oz
Cream of tartar	5 ml/1 tsp
Water	120 ml/4 fl oz
Single cream	30 ml/6 tsp
Egg yolk	1
Pinch of sea salt	

For the filling:
Quark (20% fat)	100 g/4 oz
Sunflower seeds	10 ml/2 tsp
Clear honey	10 ml/2 tsp

In addition:
Butter	20 ml/4 tsp
Flaked almonds	50 g/2 oz

1. Mix the flour with the cream of tartar. Gradually add the water, cream and egg yolk and mix to a thin batter.

2. Add a pinch of salt to the batter, cover and leave to stand for 15 minutes.

3. To make the filling, mix the quark with the sunflower seeds and honey.

4. Melt the butter in a frying pan. Add half the flaked almonds and roast. Spread thinly over the base of pan.

5. Pour in half the pancake batter and fry over a medium heat for 1-2 minutes. Turn the pancake and fry for another 1-2 minutes. Prepare the second pancake in the same way.

6. Spread the pancakes with the quark mixture, roll up and serve hot.

Preparation time: 35 mins
Serves 1
Approx. 550 kcal/2300 kJ

Protein-rich Main Meals

In this chapter, neutral foods are combined with those that belong to the proteins. For example, there are vegetable dishes covered in melted cheese (up to 50 per cent fat), delicious egg dishes and others containing poultry, meat and fish.

As in the previous chapter, there are salads for packed lunches which are easy to prepare. Also dishes made in the usual way, from meat and fish, which are generally more substantial than those in which vegetables are the most prominent, but not necessarily calorie-laden.

Meat and fish provide us with high-value protein, vitamins and trace elements – they are in no way foods which we should do without. Only the right balance is important. Over-indulgence in protein foods is not advantageous.

Courgette Soufflé

Ingredients	Metric/Imperial
Onion	1
Cold pressed olive oil	10 ml/2 tsp
Courgettes	500 g/1 lb 2 oz
Ripe tomatoes, blanched	500 g/1 lb 2 oz
Chilli powder	5 ml/1 tsp
Herbs de Provence	5 ml/1 tsp
Vegetable stock powder	10 ml/2 tsp
Garlic clove, peeled and crushed	1
Gouda cheese (45% fat), grated	150 g/5 oz

1. Peel the onion, finely chop and fry in the oil.
2. Top and tail the courgettes. Slice finely and add to the onions. Lightly fry, until golden, stirring all the time, then remove from the heat.
3. Skin the tomatoes and purée. Pass the purée through a sieve to remove the seeds.
4. Season the tomato purée with chilli powder, Provence herbs and stock powder. Crush in the peeled garlic and mix in well. Pre-heat the oven to 180°C/350°F/gas mark 4.
5. Place the courgette and onion mixture alternately in layers with the tomato sauce in a greased soufflé dish. Sprinkle with cheese.
6. Place the soufflé in the oven and bake for 20 minutes. It should form a golden yellow crust on top.
(Photo opposite top)

Preparation time: 25 mins
Cooking time: 20 mins
Serves 2
Approx. 420 kcal/1750 kJ

Apple Onion Gratin

Ingredients	Metric/Imperial
Soft dessert apples	4
Lemon juice	30 ml/2 tbsp
Red onions	400 g/14 oz
Raisins	20 ml/4 tsp
Single cream	100 ml/3½ fl oz
Pinch of cayenne pepper	
Sea salt	2.5 ml/½ tsp
Mozzarella cheese, grated	125 g/4½ oz

1. Quarter the apples, peel, remove the cores, cut into fine segments and sprinkle with lemon juice.
2. Peel the onions and cut into thin slices.
3. Place the apples, onions and raisins in a greased soufflé dish in layers. Pre-heat the oven to 200°C/400°F/gas mark 6.
4. Season the cream with the cayenne pepper and salt. Pour over the apple and onion mixture.
5. Sprinkle with the Mozzarella and bake for 45 minutes.
(Photo opposite bottom)

Preparation time: 25 mins
Baking time: 45 mins
Serves 2
Approx. 390 kcal/1605 kJ

Grilled Vegetables

Ingredients	Metric/Imperial
Mixed frozen vegetables (cauliflower, broccoli, green beans, cauliflower, etc), thawed	675 g/1½ lb

For the sauce:

Soured cream	100 ml/3½ fl oz
Single cream	100 ml/3½ fl oz
Water	150 ml/¼ pt
Vegetable stock powder	10 ml/2 tsp
Pinch of cayenne pepper	

In addition:

Parmesan cheese, grated	75 g/3 oz

1. Pre-heat the oven to 180°C/350°F/gas mark 4. Place the vegetables in a soufflé dish.
2. Make the sauce by stirring together the two creams, water, the stock powder and cayenne pepper. Beat well with a whisk and pour over the vegetables.
3. Sprinkle with the Parmesan, place the dish in the oven and bake for 15-20 minutes.
(Photo opposite centre)

Preparation time: 15 mins
Baking time: 15-20 mins
Serves 2
Approx. 445 kcal/1855 kJ

Grilled Cauliflower

Ingredients Metric/Imperial

Water	300 ml/½ pt
Vegetable stock powder	10 ml/2 tsp
Cauliflower florets	650 g/1½ lb
Gouda cheese, grated	100 g/4 oz

1. Heat the water, season with the stock powder and add the cauliflower florets. Cook over a low heat for 12-14 minutes until softened but still firm. Leave uncovered.
2. Pre-heat the oven to 200°C/400°F/gas mark 6. Remove the vegetables with a ladle, place in a soufflé dish and pour over some stock.
3. Sprinkle the cheese over the cauliflower, place the dish in the oven and bake for about 10 minutes until the cheese has melted.
(Photo bottom)

Preparation time: 30 mins
Grilling time: 10 mins
Serves 2
Approx. 305 kcal/1290 kJ

Stuffed Onions

Ingredients Metric/Imperial

Spanish onions	4
Button mushrooms	300 g/11 oz
Butter	20 ml/4 tsp
Vegetable stock powder	10 ml/2 tsp
Coriander	5 ml/1 tsp
Mild curry powder	10 ml/2 tsp
Garlic cloves	2
Gouda cheese	100 g/4 oz
Soured cream	45 ml/3 tbsp
Parsley sprig	1

1. Peel the onions and steam whole over boiling water for 10 minutes. Keep the cooking water, leave the onions to cool a little, cut a lid off each and hollow out each onion.
2. Cut the mushrooms into very thin slices. Chop the inside of the onions and the lids finely and fry in the butter with the mushrooms, for about 5 minutes or until a warm golden yellow.
3. Season lightly with the stock powder, coriander and curry. Crush the garlic and add.
4. Pre-heat the oven to 160°C/325°F/gas mark 3. Dice the cheese, add to the vegetables with the soured cream and pack into the onions. Place what is left on one side.

5. Stand the filled onions in a soufflé dish, pour over some of the water used to cook the onions and then put the rest of the filling in the dish.
6. Bake, uncovered, for about 15 minutes. Garnish with parsley.
(Photo top)

Preparation time: 1 hr
Grilling time: 15 mins
Serves 2
Approx. 335 kcal/1480 kJ

Grilled Aubergines

Ingredients Metric/Imperial

Aubergine	500 g/1 lb 2 oz
Sea salt to taste	
Tomatoes, blanched	500 g/1 lb 2 oz
Eggs	3
Parmesan cheese, grated	50 g/2 oz
Cold pressed olive oil	10 ml/2 tsp
Water	60 ml/4 tbsp
Chopped fresh thyme	5 ml/1 tsp
Chopped fresh rosemary	5 ml/1 tsp
Vegetable stock powder	10 ml/2 tsp
Garlic cloves, peeled and crushed	2
Mozzarella cheese	125 g/4½ oz

1. Remove the stalk from the aubergine and cut the fruit into 5mm/¼ in thick slices.
2. Salt each slice lightly on both sides, place in a sieve and leave to stand for about 30 minutes.
3. Skin and purée the tomatoes and pass through a sieve to remove the seeds.
4. Whisk the eggs until foamy and add to the tomato purée. Mix in the Parmesan cheese, oil, water, thyme, rosemary and stock powder. Add the garlic cloves and mix thoroughly.
5. Pre-heat the oven to 180°C/350°F/gas mark 4. Dry the aubergine slices. Lay them alternately in a round heat resistant dish with the tomato sauce.
6. Slice the Mozzarella cheese and place on top of the aubergine. Bake for about 50 minutes. If the cheese browns too much, cover the dish with a piece of foil.
(Photo centre)

Preparation time: 30 mins
Grilling time: 50 mins
Serves 2
Approx. 595 kcal/2490 kJ

Farmer's Fry

Ingredients	Metric/Imperial
Small leek	1
Mushrooms	100 g/4 oz
Small red pepper	1
Butter	10 ml/2 tsp
Vegetable stock powder	5 ml/1 tsp
Paprika	5 ml/1 tsp
Sheep's cheese	50 g/2 oz
Eggs	2
Single cream	20 ml/4 tsp
Mineral water	45 ml/3 tbsp
Chopped fresh chives	15 ml/1 tbsp
Tomato	1
Pitted black olives	4

1. Clean the leek, wipe the mushrooms with a damp cloth and slice both thinly.
2. De-seed the pepper and cut the flesh into fine strips.
3. Melt the butter in a frying pan, add the vegetables and fry for 5 minutes until just soft. Mix in the stock powder and paprika. Crumble the cheese and sprinkle over the vegetables.
4. Separate the eggs. Beat the egg whites until stiff and stir in the yolks with the cream and the mineral water.

5. Pour the mixture over the vegetables then cover the pan.
6. Leave the egg to set over a low heat for about 10 minutes.
7. Sprinkle the farmer's fry with the chopped chives. Cut the tomato into 8 and garnish the dish with the tomato slices and the olives.
(Photo top)

Preparation time: 45 mins
Serves 1
Approx. 640 kcal/2685 kJ

Vegetable Omelette

Ingredients	Metric/Imperial
Red pepper	1
Onion	1
Cold pressed sunflower oil	10 ml/2 tsp
Eggs	2
Water	20 ml/4 tsp
Single cream	20 ml/4 tsp
Sea salt	2.5 ml/½ tsp
Paprika	2.5 ml/½ tsp
Chopped fresh chives	20 ml/4 tsp

1. De-seed the pepper and cut the flesh into fine strips. Peel the onion and finely chop.
2. Heat the oil in a frying pan and gently fry the pepper strips and onion for 5 minutes. Spread the vegetables evenly over the base of the pan.
3. Whisk the eggs with the water and cream then season with the salt and paprika.
4. Stir in the chopped chives and pour the egg mixture into the frying pan. Cook over a low heat until the eggs set, keeping the pan half covered.
5. Slide the omelette on to a plate and eat hot.
(Photo bottom)

Preparation time: 20 mins
Serves 1
Approx. 385 kcal/1620 kJ

Note
Accompany with a salad or neutral food

Scrambled Eggs with Warm Vegetable Salad

Ingredients Metric/Imperial

For the salad:

Yellow pepper	1
Red pepper	1
Carrots	2
Celeriac	150 g/5 oz
Large leek	1
Vegetable stock	300 ml/½ pt
Bay leaf	1
Garlic clove, peeled	1
Chopped fresh thyme	5 ml/1 tsp

For the sauce:

Single cream	50 g/2 oz
Soy sauce	10 ml/2 tsp
Chopped mixed fresh herbs (parsley, chervil, tarragon)	30 ml/2 tbsp
Herb salt	5 ml/1 tsp
Pinch of saffron	

For the scrambled eggs:

Eggs	3
Mineral water	40 ml/2½ tbsp
Single cream	20 ml/4 tsp
Butter	10 ml/2 tsp

In addition:

Chopped fresh chives	30 ml/2 tbsp

1. De-seed the peppers and cut the flesh into thin strips.

2. Peel the carrots and the celeriac, clean the leek and finely chop all three.

3. Heat the stock and add the bay leaf, the whole garlic clove and the thyme. Cook the vegetables in the stock for 8-10 minutes until just firm to the bite. Keep the pan covered and the heat moderate.

4. Remove the vegetables from the pan with a draining spoon, discard the bay leaf and the garlic clove and keep the vegetables warm on a plate. Leave 100 ml/ 3½ fl oz of the stock to cool.

5. To make the sauce, stir the cream together with the soy sauce and the cooled stock. Add the herbs, season with herb salt and the saffron and pour over the vegetables.

6. Whisk the eggs with the mineral water, cream and herb salt.

7. Melt the butter in a frying pan, pour in the egg mixture and leave to set over a low heat, stirring constantly until lightly scrambled.

8. Serve the scrambled eggs with the vegetable salad and sprinkle with chives.

Preparation time: 45 mins
Serves 2
Approx. 425 kcal/1785 kJ

Turkey Roll with Leek Almond Vegetables

Ingredients Metric/Imperial

For the vegetables:

Leeks	4
Onions	4
Butter	10 ml/2 tsp
Vegetable stock powder	10 ml/2 tsp
Nutmeg	2.5 ml/½ tsp
Flaked almonds	40 g/1½ oz
Single cream	30 ml/2 tbsp

For the rolls:

Turkey steaks each 150g/5 oz	2
Butter	15 ml/1 tbsp
Water	200 ml/7 fl oz

For the sauce:

Arrowroot or potato starch	10 ml/2 tsp
Water	15 ml/1 tbsp

1. Clean the leeks, peel the onions and cut both into very fine slices.
2. Melt the butter in a frying pan, add the leek and the onions and fry gently for 4 minutes.
3. Season the vegetables with half the stock powder and nutmeg, then mix in the almonds and the cream.

4. Beat the turkey steaks flat, wash and wipe dry and spread evenly with some of the vegetable mixture.
5. Roll up and hold in place with two skewers or cocktails sticks.
6. Heat the butter in a small frying pan. Add the turkey rolls and brown quickly. Pour over the water and cook, covered, over a low heat for 20-25 minutes.

7. Season the sauce with the rest of the stock powder then stir in the arrowroot or potato flour smoothly mixed with cold water. Bring slowly to the boil, stirring, and simmer 1-2 minutes until thickened.
8. Heat up the rest of the vegetable mixture and serve with the turkey rolls and sauce.

Preparation time: 1 hr
Serves 2
Approx. 560 kcal/2355 kJ

Swiss Bean Salad

Ingredients	Metric/Imperial
Green beans	300 g/11 oz
Sea salt to taste	

For the sauce:

Thick yoghurt	120 ml/4 fl oz
Soy sauce	5 ml/1 tsp
Herb salt	2.5 ml/½ tsp
Small onion	1
Frozen sweet corn, thawed	100 g/4 oz

In addition:

Swiss Emmenthal or Gruyère cheese	50 g/2 oz
Chopped walnuts	20 ml/4 tsp

1. String the beans and cut into pieces about 3 cm/1¼ in long. Cook in lightly salted water for 10 minutes until firm to the bite.
2. For the sauce, mix together the yoghurt, soy sauce and the herb salt.
3. Drain the beans and leave to cool. Peel the onion, finely chop and add to the sauce with the sweet corn.
4. Combine the sauce with the beans. Cut the cheese into fine strips, place in the middle of the salad and sprinkle with chopped nuts.
(Photo opposite top)

Preparation time: 40 mins
Serves 1
Approx. 750 kcal/3130 kJ

Tomato Salad and Scrambled Eggs

Ingredients	Metric/Imperial

For the salad:

Cold pressed sunflower oil	10 ml/2 tsp
Soy sauce	10 ml/2 tsp
Water	200 ml/7 fl oz
Herb salt	5 ml/1 tsp
Onion	1
Tomatoes	8
Chopped fresh parsley	30 ml/2 tbsp

For the scrambled eggs:

Eggs	3
Mineral water	45 ml/3 tbsp
Single cream	20 ml/4 tsp
Sea salt	2.5 ml/½ tsp
Onion	½
Butter	10 ml/2 tsp
Chopped fresh chives	30 ml/1 tbsp

1. For the salad, stir together the sunflower oil, soy sauce, water and herb salt.
2. Dice the onion very finely and add half to the above mixture.
3. Thinly slice the tomatoes. Arrange on a plate, pour over the sauce and sprinkle with parsley.
4. Beat the eggs with the mineral water, the cream and the sea salt.
5. Fry the rest of the onion in the butter until clear. Add the egg mixture and stir over a low heat until scrambled.
6. Sprinkle the scrambled eggs with chives. Serve with the salad.
(Photo opposite centre)

Preparation time: 25 mins
Serves 2
Approx. 430 kcal/1815 kJ

Variation
If you like you can add strips of cooked beef to the eggs while scrambling.

Turkey Cream Steaks with Beans

Ingredients	Metric/Imperial
Butter	10 ml/2 tsp
Water	150 ml/¼ pt
Green beans	450 g/1 lb
Dried savoury	5 ml/1 tsp
Vegetable stock powder	10 ml/2 tsp
Turkey steaks, each 150g/5 oz	2
Herb salt	5 ml/1 tsp
Butter	10 ml/2 tsp
Single cream	75 ml/5 tbsp
Water	45 ml/3 tbsp
Green peppercorns	10 ml/2 tsp

1. Melt the butter in a saucepan, then add the water and the beans.
2. Stir in the savoury and the stock powder and leave to simmer in a closed saucepan for 7-10 minutes, stirring occasionally.
3. Wash the turkey steaks, pat dry and season with a little herb salt.
4. Warm the fat in a frying pan, add the turkey steaks and fry on each side for 5 minutes. Remove to a plate and keep hot.
5. Drain the beans and keep warm.
6. Mix the cream with water and pour into the pan in which turkey was frying. Add the peppercorns.
7. Reheat until hot, adjust seasoning to taste and pour over steaks. Accompany with the beans.
(Photo opposite bottom)

Preparation time: 25 mins
Serves 2
Approx. 520 kcal/2190 kJ

Waldorf Chicken Salad

Ingredients Metric/Imperial

Chicken breast fillets	2
Water	450 ml/¾ pt
Vegetable stock powder	5 ml/1 tsp
Celeriac	75 g/3 oz
Carrots	2
Tart apples	2
Lemon juice	20 ml/2 tsp
Fresh pineapple	½
Walnut halves	6

For the sauce:

Thick yoghurt	200 ml/7 fl oz
Glucose syrup	5 ml/1 tsp
Soy sauce	10 ml/2 tsp
Herb salt	5 ml/1 tsp

1. Rinse the chicken breasts. Bring the water to the boil in a saucepan, stir in the stock powder, add the chicken and simmer for 20-25 minutes.
2. Peel the celeriac and cook until just tender in a little water. Leave to cool then cut into strips.
3. Remove the chicken meat from the stock, cut into pieces and leave to cool.
4. Peel the carrots and cut into fine strips. Quarter the apples, remove cores and cut into strips. Mix with the lemon juice.

5. Peel the pineapple, remove the brown eyes and cut the flesh into small pieces. Chop the nuts coarsely. Mix all the ingredients well together.
6. To make the sauce, stir the yoghurt with the syrup, soy sauce and the herb salt. Add to the salad ingredients and toss well to mix.
(Photo left)

Preparation time: 1 hr
Serves 2
Approx. 600 kcal/2525 kJ

Chicken Salad and Lentil Sprouts

Ingredients Metric/Imperial

Cucumber	1
Corn salad	75 g/3 oz
Tomatoes	5
Chicken breast fillets	2
Sea salt	5 ml/1 tsp
Cold pressed sunflower oil	20 ml/4 tsp

For the sauce:

Onion	1
Soy sauce	10 ml/2 tsp
Glucose syrup	5 ml/1 tsp
Vegetable stock	100ml/3½ fl oz
Chopped fresh dill	20 ml/4 tsp
Soured cream	30 ml/2 tbsp

In addition:

Lentil sprouts (home-grown, see page 21 or bought)	150 g/5 oz

1. Peel the cucumber, halve lengthways and scrape out seeds with a spoon. Cut the remainder into slices.
2. Clean the corn salad and cut each tomato into 8 segments. Arrange, with the cucumber, on 2 plates.
3. Lightly salt the chicken breast fillets. Fry in the oil in a frying pan for about 5 minutes per side.
4. To make the sauce, peel the onion, chop finely and combine with the soy sauce, syrup and stock.
5. Stir in chopped dill and soured cream. Mix thoroughly.
6. Cut the chicken breast fillets into strips while still warm and arrange on top of the salad. Coat with the sauce and sprinkle with lentil sprouts.
(Photo right)

Preparation time: 45 mins
Serves 2
Approx. 580 kcal/2440 kJ

Rissoles with Vegetables

Ingredients Metric/Imperial

For the rissoles:

Carrot	1
Onion	1
Minced steak	150 g/5 oz
Egg yolk	1
Herb salt	5 ml /1 tsp
Finely chopped fresh herbs (parsley, thyme, marjoram)	20 ml/4 tsp
Butter	10 ml/2 tsp

For the vegetables:

Spring onions	3
Carrots	3
Courgette	1
Butter	10 ml/2 tsp
Water	50 ml/2 fl oz
Vegetable stock powder	5 ml/1 tsp

In addition:

Chopped fresh parsley	10 ml/2 tsp

1. Peel the carrot and grate finely. Peel the onion and finely chop.
2. Place the minced steak in a bowl and mix with the egg yolk, herb salt, onion, carrot and the herbs. Stand for about 10 minutes, covered.
3. Clean the spring onions and cut into rings. Peel the carrots and cut into thin diagonal slices. Top and tail the courgette and thinly slice.
4. Gently fry the vegetables in the melted butter. Add the water and season with the stock powder. Cover the pan and simmer for 10-15 minutes.
5. Shape the meat mixture into rissoles and fry in the hot fat until both sides are brown and the centres are cooked through. Keep the heat moderate and allow about 7-8 minutes, turning twice.
6. Serve the rissoles with the vegetables and sprinkle with parsley.
(Photo opposite top)

Preparation time: 40 mins
Serves 1
Approx. 520 kcal/2165 kJ

Stuffed Braised Marrow

Ingredients Metric/Imperial

Medium marrow	1
Onion	1
Cold pressed sunflower oil	10 ml/2 tsp
Garlic cloves, peeled	2
Minced steak	250 g/9 oz
Ripe tomatoes	8
Herb salt	10 ml/2 tsp
Herbs de Provence	10 ml/2 tsp
Vegetable stock powder	10 ml/2 tsp
Pinch of cayenne pepper	
Single cream	30 ml/2 tbsp
Chopped fresh basil	10 ml/2 tsp

1. Peel the marrow, halve lengthways and carefully remove the seeds with a spoon.
2. Peel the onion, chop finely and fry gently in the oil until transparent. Crush in the garlic.
3. Add the minced meat and stir-fry, stirring with a fork, until brown and crumbly.
4. Blanch and skin the tomatoes and cut into quarters. Work to a purée and sieve to remove the seeds.
5. Add 75 ml/5 tbsp of tomato purée to the minced meat and season with herb salt and Provence herbs. Fill the marrow halves with the minced meat filling.
6. Put the rest of the tomato purée in a flameproof dish, season with stock powder and cayenne pepper and arrange in the stuffed marrow on top.
7. Cover and cook on a low heat for about 30 minutes. Stir in the cream and serve the marrows garnished with basil. Spoon the sauce around each half.
(Photo opposite bottom)

Preparation time: 1 hr
Serves 2
Approx. 555 kcal/2315 kJ

Spinach and Minced Meat Bake

Ingredients Metric/Imperial

Onion	1
Butter	10 ml/2 tsp
Minced steak	250 g/9 oz
Herb salt	5 ml/1 tsp
Pinch of cayenne pepper	
Pinch of grated nutmeg	
Frozen leaf spinach, thawed	575 g/15 oz
Single cream	150 ml/¼ pt
Water	100ml/3½ floz
Parmesan cheese, grated	50 g/2 oz

1. Peel the onion, chop finely and fry until clear in butter.
2. Add the minced meat and fry for 5 minutes, fork-stirring continuously. Season with herb salt, cayenne pepper and nutmeg. Pre-heat the oven to 180°C/350°F/gas mark 4.
3. Arrange half of the spinach in a heat-resistant dish and place half the minced meat on top. Add the rest of the spinach and finally the rest of the minced meat.
4. Mix the cream with water, stir in the Parmesan cheese and pour over the soufflé. Bake for about 20 minutes.
(Photo opposite centre)

Preparation time: 25 mins
Cooking time: 20 mins
Serves 2
Approx. 750 kcal/3120 kJ

Leek Casserole

Ingredients — Metric/Imperial

Ingredients	Metric/Imperial
Large leeks	4
Vegetable stock powder	5 ml/1 tsp
Onions	2
Soft margarine	10 ml/2 tsp
Minced steak	200 g/7 oz
Tomatoes	4
Paprika	10 ml/2 tsp
Water	150 ml/¼ pt
Pinch of coriander	
Garlic clove, peeled	1
Chopped fresh rosemary	5 ml/1 tsp
Chopped fresh thyme	5 ml/1 tsp
Single cream	45 ml/3 tbsp
Cheddar cheese, grated	60 g/2½ oz

1. Clean the leeks and cut into fine rings. Place in a saucepan, just cover with water, add the stock powder and cook for about 20 minutes over a moderate heat.

2. Peel the onions, dice and fry in the margarine until clear. Separate the minced meat, add to the onions and fry for 5-6 minutes, stirring until brown and crumbly.

3. Blanch the tomatoes in boiling water, remove the skins and chop.

4. Add to the minced meat with the paprika. Pour over the water and simmer for about 10 minutes.

5. Pre-heat the oven to 180°C/350°F/gas mark 4. Stir the coriander into the minced meat mixture then crush in the garlic. Season everything with rosemary and thyme and stir in the cream.

6. Drain the leeks and place in a heatproof dish. Arrange the minced meat on top and sprinkle with cheese. Bake for 15-20 minutes until brown. *(Photo top)*

Preparation time: 1 hr
Baking time: 20 mins
Serves 2
Approx. 520 kcal/2145 kJ

Moussaka

Ingredients — Metric/Imperial

Ingredients	Metric/Imperial
Aubergines	2
Sea salt to taste	
Cold pressed olive oil	60 ml/4 tbsp
Garlic cloves, peeled and crushed	2
Minced steak	300 g/11 oz
Onion	1
Red pepper	1
Green pepper	1
Tomatoes	4
Vegetable stock	150 ml/¼ pt
Small bay leaf	1
Small sprig thyme	1
Sea salt to taste	
Paprika	5 ml/1 tsp
Chopped parsley	20 ml/4 tsp

1. Clean the aubergines and cut into slices about 1 cm/½ in thick. Sprinkle with salt, place in a sieve and leave for about 10 minutes. Rinse and drain.

2. Wipe the aubergine slices dry with paper towels.

3. Heat the oil in a frying pan, add garlic and the aubergine slices and fry until golden yellow. Remove from pan and drain on crumpled kitchen paper.

4. Add the minced meat to the remaining fat in the frying pan and stir-fry until crumbly. Peel the onion and chop. Add to the meat and fry together for about 5 minutes.

5. De-seed the peppers and cut flesh into dice. Add to the meat and fry for 5 minutes.

6. Blanch the tomatoes in boiling water, remove the skins and dice. Mix into the minced meat.

7. Add the vegetable stock, the bay leaf and the thyme sprig and bring to the boil. Pre-heat the oven to 180°C/350°F/gas mark 4.

8. Season the minced meat with salt and paprika and simmer for 10-15 minutes in a half covered pan. Remove the bay leaf.

9. Place half the aubergine slices in a large greased casserole dish and spread the minced meat sauce evenly on top.

10. Place the rest of the aubergine slices on top and bake for 20 minutes. Before serving, sprinkle with parsley. *(Photo bottom)*

Preparation time: 1 hr
Baking time: 20 mins
Serves 2
Approx. 700 kcal/2930 kJ

Minced Beef Pot

Ingredients	Metric/Imperial
Spanish onions	2
Red peppers	3
Butter	20 ml/4 tsp
Minced beef	250 g/9 oz
Paprika	10 ml/2 tsp
Tomatoes, blanched and skinned	8
Garlic cloves, peeled and crushed	2
Oregano	5 ml/1 tsp
Vegetable stock powder	10 ml/2 tsp
Single cream	45 ml/3 tbsp

1. Peel the onions and cut into thin slices. De-seed the peppers and cut the flesh into fine strips.
2. Lightly fry the onions and pepper strips in the butter. Separate the minced meat with a fork, add to the pan and fry for 5 minutes, stirring all the time. Season with paprika.
3. Quarter the tomatoes and purée. Pass through a sieve to remove the seeds.
4. Add the purée to the minced meat with the garlic.
5. Season with oregano and the stock powder, cover and simmer for about 10 minutes in a closed saucepan. Finally, stir in the cream.
(Photo centre)

Preparation time: 45 mins
Serves 2
Approx. 625 kcal/2615 kJ

Stuffed Peppers

Ingredients	Metric/Imperial
Red peppers	4
Carrots	2
Large onion	1
Egg	1
Minced beef	275 g/10 oz
Pinch of cayenne pepper	
Herb salt	5 ml/1 tsp
Mushrooms	200 g/7 oz
Cold pressed olive oil	10 ml/2 tsp
Vegetable stock	300 ml/½ pt
Arrowroot or potato starch	15 ml/1 tbsp
Water	15 ml/1 tbsp
Single cream	45 ml/3 tbsp
Basil sprig	1

1. Cut a lid off the top of each pepper and remove the seeds. Cut a thin slice away from the base of each so that the peppers will stand upright without toppling.
2. Chop up the pepper lids. Peel the carrots and grate finely.
3. Peel and halve the onion. Chop one half very finely and add to the minced meat with the egg and carrot.
4. Mix well and season the meat mixture with cayenne pepper and herb salt. Spoon into the peppers.
5. Slice the mushrooms. Cut the remaining half an onion into thin slices.
6. Heat the oil in a frying pan over a medium heat, add the mushrooms and onion and fry lightly for about 4 minutes.
7. Stand the filled peppers in a deep saucepan, add the fried vegetables then pour on the vegetable stock. Cover and simmer gently for about 45 minutes to 1 hour when the peppers should be tender. Remove to a plate and keep hot.
8. To thicken the sauce, mix the arrowroot or potato starch smoothly with the water and cream.
9. Add to the pan juices and bring to the boil. Simmer for 2 minutes. Coat peppers with the sauce then garnish with basil leaves cut into strips. (Photo top)

Preparation time: 1¼ hrs
Serves 2
Approx. 545 kcal/2280 kJ

Hungarian Goulash

Ingredients	Metric/Imperial
Lean rump steak	275 g/9 oz
Spanish onion	1
Red pepper	1
Green pepper	1
Soft margarine	10 ml/2 tsp
Paprika	20 ml/4 tsp
Pinch of cayenne pepper	
Ripe tomatoes, blanched	1 kg/2 lb
Garlic cloves, peeled and crushed	2
Chopped fresh coriander	5 ml/1 tsp
Chopped fresh rosemary	5 ml/1 tsp
Chopped fresh thyme	5 ml/1 tsp
Caraway seeds	5 ml/1 tsp
Bay leaves	2
Vegetable stock powder	20 ml/4 tsp
Single cream	45 ml/3 tbsp

1. Wash and dry the steak and cut into cubes. Peel the onion and cut into slices.
2. De-seed the peppers and cut the flesh into narrow strips.
3. Heat the margarine in a frying pan, add the meat cubes and fry for 5 minutes. Add the onion rings and fry until transparent.
4. Add the pepper strips and season with paprika and cayenne pepper.
5. Skin and chop the tomatoes then pass through a sieve to remove the seeds.
6. Add to the meat mixture. Add the garlic then stir in the herbs, bay leaves and stock powder.
7. Cover and simmer for 1 hour, stirring from time to time. Before serving, remove the bay leaves and stir in the cream.
(Photo bottom)

Preparation time: 1½ hrs
Serves 2
Approx. 565 kcal/2375 kJ

Polish-Style Borsch

Ingredients	Metric/Imperial
Onion	1
Butter	15 ml/1 tbsp
Lean lamb	275 g/10 oz
Button mushrooms	150 g/5 oz
Caraway seeds	5 ml/1 tsp
Bay leaf	1
Juniper berries	3
Vegetable stock	450 ml/¾ pt
White cabbage	400 g/14 oz
Beetroot	200 g/7 oz
Soured cream	30 ml/2 tbsp

1. Peel the onion, cut into rings and fry until soft in the butter.
2. Wash the meat, pat dry, cut into cubes and add to the onions.
3. Clean the mushrooms, add to the pan and fry for 5 minutes, turning. Stir in caraway seeds, the bay leaf and the juniper berries. Add the vegetable stock, bring to the boil and cover. Simmer for 30 minutes.
4. Clean the cabbage and cut into thin shreds. Peel the beetroot and cut into thin slices.
5. Add the white cabbage and beetroot to the pan of meat and simmer in a closed saucepan over a moderate heat for about 20 minutes.
6. Add soured cream to each portion.
(Photo opposite top)

Preparation time: 1¼ hrs
Serves 2
Approx. 370 kcal/1550 kJ

Fish Soup

Ingredients	Metric/Imperial
Ripe tomatoes	8
Leek	1
Carrots	2
Shellfish or cod fillet	400 g/14 oz
Vegetable stock powder	15 ml/1 tbsp
Pinch of cayenne pepper	
Single cream	50 g/2 oz
Chopped fresh parsley	20 ml/4 tsp

1. Blanch, skin and chop the tomatoes.
2. Pass through a sieve to remove the seeds and place the purée in a saucepan.
3. Clean the leek and cut into fine rings. Peel the carrots and dice finely. Add both to the tomato purée and leave to simmer for about 8 minutes.
4. Wash the fish, remove any fine bones and cut into pieces.
5. Add the fish pieces to the soup and season with the stock powder and cayenne pepper. Leave to simmer for 8-10 minutes in a half-covered pan.
6. Stir in the cream and sprinkle the soup with parsley.
(Photo opposite centre)

Preparation time: 50 mins
Serves 2
Approx. 305 kcal/1270 kJ

Salmon Fillet with Mixed Vegetables

Ingredients	Metric/Imperial
Cauliflower	250 g/9 oz
Broccoli	250 g/9 oz
Carrots	2
Water	300 ml/½ pt
Sea salt	5 ml/1 tsp
Salmon fillets, each 150 g/5 oz	2
Herb salt	5 ml/1 tsp
Cold pressed sunflower oil	20 ml/4 tsp
Butter	15 ml/1 tbsp

1. Divide the cauliflower and the broccoli into small florets. Peel the broccoli stalks, quarter along the length and cut into pieces.
2. Peel the carrots and slice thinly.
3. Bring the carrots to the boil in the lightly salted water, add the broccoli stalks first and cook for about 5 minutes. Afterwards add the rest of the vegetables and simmer for a further 8-10 minutes.
4. Wash the salmon fillets, then dry and lightly season with the herb salt. Fry in oil for about 8 minutes over a medium heat, turning twice.
5. Remove the vegetables from the water with a ladle and leave to drain. Gently brown the butter in a frying pan, stir into the vegetables and serve with the fish.
(Photo opposite bottom)

Preparation time: 45 mins
Serves 2
Approx. 530 kcal/2225 kJ

Fish Ratatouille

Ingredients	Metric/Imperial
Aubergine	200 g/7 oz
Red peppers	2
Courgette	1
Onions	2
Cold pressed olive oil	20 ml/4 tsp
Tomatoes	6
Garlic cloves, peeled and crushed	2
Herbes de Provence	5 ml/1 tsp
Vegetable stock powder	10 ml/2 tsp
Fish fillets	400 g/14 oz
Single cream	45 ml/3 tbsp
Dash of white wine	
Chopped fresh parsley	20 ml/4 tsp

1. Clean the aubergine, pepper, courgette and onions. Cut into equal sized dice. Fry the vegetables one after another in the olive oil over a moderate heat.
2. Blanch and peel the tomatoes then chop and purée. Pass through a sieve to remove the seeds then add to the vegetables with the garlic.
3. Season the vegetables with the Provence herbs and the stock powder.
4. Wash the fish fillets, pat dry and cut into 12 pieces of equal size. Add this to the vegetables. Gently stir and simmer in a closed saucepan for 6-8 minutes.
5. Carefully fold in the cream and season the dish with wine. Sprinkle with parsley.
(Photo bottom)

Preparation time: 40 mins
Serves 2
Approx. 425 kcal/1780 kJ

Plaice in Orange Cream Sauce

Ingredients	Metric/Imperial
Plaice fillets	400 g/14 oz
Herb salt	5 ml/1 tsp
Butter	20 ml/4 tsp
Freshly squeezed orange juice	150 ml/¼ pt
Pinch of cayenne pepper	
Single cream	45 ml/3 tbsp

1. Wash the plaice fillets, pat dry and season with the herb salt.
2. Melt the butter in a frying pan and fry the fish on both sides for 4-5 minutes, turning once. Transfer to a plate and keep hot.
3. Add the orange juice to the pan juices, season lightly and stir in the cayenne pepper and cream.
(Photo centre)

Preparation time: 20 mins
Serves 2
Approx. 365 kcal/1525 kJ

Note
As a starter, serve a salad, such as a fennel salad (see page 54).

Blue Trout

Ingredients	Metric/Imperial
Water	1¼ l/2¼ pts
Carrot	1
Onion	1
Bay leaf	1
Lemon juice	5 ml/1 tsp
Large filleted trout	1
Herb salt	5 ml/1 tsp

1. Bring the water to the boil. Peel the carrot and the onion and chop. Add to the water with the bay leaf.
2. Season the cooking water with lemon juice and cook for another 20 minutes.
3. Wash the inside of the trout carefully, trying not to damage the delicate skin of the fish.
4. Sprinkle the trout with some lemon juice and lightly season with herb salt.
5. Remove the cooking stock from the heat and slide the trout into it. Leave to cook in the hot stock for 8-10 minutes. Additional heating will be unnecessary and the skin should automatically turn blue, especially if the trout has been freshly caught and is wild rather than farmed.
(Photo top)

Preparation time: 45 mins
Serves 1
Approx. 180 kcal/750 kJ

Note
Eat with cooked vegetables or a large salad.

Fish Dish

Ingredients	Metric/Imperial
Red pepper	1
Leek	1
Carrot	1
Butter	10 ml/2 tsp
Vegetable stock	100ml/3½ floz
Red mullet fillets, skinned	2
Lemon juice	10 ml/2 tsp
Herb salt	5 ml/1 tsp
Arrowroot or potato flour (optional)	15 ml/1 tbsp
Cold water	15 ml/1 tbsp
Single cream	20 ml/4 tsp
Parsley sprigs	3
Lemon slices	2

1. De-seed pepper and chop. Clean the leek, peel the carrot and slice both thinly.
2. Melt the butter in a large frying pan, add the vegetables and fry gently for 7 minutes. Add the vegetable stock, cover and cook for 5 minutes.
3. Wash the fish fillets and dry. Dice, sprinkle with lemon juice and season with herb salt.
4. Move the vegetables to the edge of the pan, place the fish in the centre and fry for 6-8 minutes. Turn the fish once.

5. Transfer fish to a plate and keep hot. Mix the arrowroot or potato flour smoothly with cold water and add to the pan juices with the cream. Bring to the boil and simmer until sauce has thickened. Serve with the fish then garnish with parsley and lemon slices.
(Photo top)

Preparation time: 50 mins
Serves 1
Approx. 430 kcal/1805 kJ

Mixed Salad with Salmon

Ingredients	Metric/Imperial
Green beans	200 g/7 oz
Sea salt to taste	
Yellow pepper	1
Tomato, blanched	1
Onion	1
Small lettuce	1

For the sauce:

Cold pressed olive oil	15 ml/1 tbsp
Soy sauce	15 ml/1 tbsp
Water	120 ml/4 fl oz
Single cream	45 ml/3 tbsp
Chopped fresh parsley	30 ml/2 tbsp
Herb salt	5 ml/1 tsp

In addition:

Olives	8
Smoked salmon	125 g/4½ oz
Hard-boiled egg	1

1. Clean and string the beans and cut into pieces about 4 cm/1½ in long.
2. Cook the beans lightly in salted water for about 8 minutes. Drain and cool.
3. De-seed the pepper and chop. Skin the tomato and chop.
4. Peel the onion, cut into fine rings and blanch quickly in boiling water.
5. Rinse the lettuce and tear into pieces then thoroughly drain. Transfer to a bowl with rest of vegetables and mix well.
6. Beat the olive oil with the soy sauce, water and the cream. Add the chopped parsley and season with the herb salt.
7. Pour the sauce over the salad and arrange the olives on top. Cut the salmon into fine strips and cut the egg into 8 pieces. Place on top of the salad.
(Photo centre)

Preparation time: 25 mins
Serves 2
Approx. 360 kcal/1505 kJ

Plaice Fillets with Cucumber Salad

Ingredients	Metric/Imperial
Plaice fillets	400 g/14 oz
Herb salt	5 ml/1 tsp
Butter	20 ml/4 tsp
Cucumber	1

For the sauce:

Soy sauce	10 ml/2 tsp
Water	200ml/7½floz
Single cream	30 ml/2 tbsp
Sea salt	2.5 ml/½ tsp
Glucose syrup	2.5 ml/½ tsp
Chopped fresh dill	20 ml/4 tsp

In addition:

Tomatoes	2

1. Wash the plaice fillets, pat dry and salt lightly.
2. Melt the butter in a frying pan and fry the fish on both sides for 6-8 minutes, turning once.
3. Peel the cucumber and slice very thinly.
4. Beat the soy sauce with the water, cream, salt, syrup and dill and mix with the cucumber slices.
5. Cut each tomato into 8 segments. Serve the plaice fillets with the cucumber salad and tomatoes.
(Photo bottom)

Preparation time: 25 mins
Serves 2
Approx. 360 kcal/1505 kJ

Index to Recipes

Almonds Biscuits 36
Almond Pancakes 99
Apple Cake 32
Apple Onion Gratin 102
Apple Purée, Semolina Dumplings with 98
Asparagus Soup 60
Aubergines, Grilled 105

Banana, Coppa 31
Bean Salad, Mexican 52
Bean Salad, Swiss 110
Bean Sprout Salad, Mixed 48
Bean Sprouts, Summer Salad with 48
Beetroot Salad 51
Berry Dessert 45
Biscuits, Almond 36
Biscuits, Four Corn 38
Biscuits, Savoury Cheese 39
Biscuits, Wholemeal Cinnamon 36
Blueberries, Cream Ice with 30
Blueberries, Oat Flakes with 28
Blueberry Mix 31
Borsch, Polish-Style 121
Bread, Mixed Pizza 94
Bread, Pick-You-Up Roll 27
Bread, Radish 27
Bread with Carrot Slices, Quark 26
Bread with Savoury Soft Cheese 28
Bread with Topping 26
Brussels Sprouts, Fried Potatoes with 72
Buttermilk Dessert, Fruity 43
Buttermilk Drink 30

Cabbage, Bavarian Caraway 52
Cabbage Soup, Pepper and 63
Carrot and Pear Salad 56
Carrot and Potato Stew 68
Cauliflower, Grilled 104
Cauliflower and Mushrooms, Wheaten 96
Cauliflower Salad, Raw 52
Celeriac Salad 57
Celeriac Soup, Cream of 62
Celery Salad, Fennel and 56
Cheese, Bread with Savoury Soft 28
Cheese, Grapefruit with Soft 40
Cheese, Wheat Salad with Sheep's 96
Cheese Biscuits, Savoury 39

Cheese Dumplings, Vegetable Soup with 77
Cheese Filling, Pancake with Goat's 94
Cheese Gratin, Potato 91
Cheese Salad, Alpine Vegetable 56
Cherry Soup, Middle European Iced 45
Chicken Salad, Waldorf 112
Chicken Salad and Lentil Sprouts 112
Corn Dumplings with Sauerkraut 95
Courgette and Potato Soup 66
Courgette Soufflé 102
Cream Ice with Blueberries 30
Cucumber Salad, Plaice Fillets with 125
Custard and Quark Pudding 28

Dumplings, Vegetable Soup with Cheese 77
Dumplings with Apple Purée, Semolina 98
Dumplings with Sauerkraut, Corn 95

Eggs, Scrambled with Tomato and Salad 110
Eggs, Scrambled with Warm Vegetable Salad 108

Farmer's Fry 107
Fennel and Celery Salad 56
Fennel Salad with Fruit 54
Fish Dish 124
Fish Ratatouille 122
Fish Soup 121
Fruity Buttermilk Dessert 43
Fruity Raw Food Platter 55

Goulash, Hungarian 118
Grapefruit, Filled 40
Grapefruit with Soft Cheese 40

Herring Salad, German 75
Herrings, Potato Salad with 74
Herrings in Cream with Potatoes 72
Honey Bars 34

Leek Almond Vegetables, Turkey Roll with 109
Leek Casserole 116
Leek Soup, Potato and 66

Macaroni Napoli 82
Marrow, Stuffed Braised 115
Melon Cocktail 43

Millet Soup	60
Minced Beef Pot	117
Minced Meat Bake, Spinach and	115
Moussaka	116
Muesli, Crunch	29
Mushroom Fry, Vegetable and	84
Mushroom Risotto	84
Mushroom Sauce, Pasta with Paprika and	78
Mushrooms au Gratin	86
Mushrooms, Pasta Salad with	83
Mushrooms, Rice with Mixed	84
Mushrooms, Wheaten Cauliflower and	96
Oat Flake Burgers with Garlic	91
Oat Flake Medallions	36
Oat Flakes with Blueberries	28
Omelette, Vegetable	107
Onion Flan	93
Onion Gratin, Apple	102
Onions, Stuffed	105
Pancake with Goat's Cheese Filling	94
Pancake Strip Soup	58
Pancakes, Almond	99
Paprika Cream Soup	59
Pasta with Paprika and Mushroom Sauce	78
Pasta Salad with Mushrooms	83
Pear Salad, Carrot and	56
Pepper and Cabbage Soup	63
Peppers, Stuffed	118
Pineapple Dessert	42
Pineapple Yoghurt	40
Pizza Bread, Mixed	94
Pizza Romana	92
Plaice Fillets with Cucumber Salad	125
Plaice in Orange Cream Sauce	122
Potato Cheese Gratin	91
Potato and Leek Soup	66
Potato Salad with Herrings	74
Potato with Sauerkraut and Fried Onion, Mashed	72
Potato Soup, Courgette and	66
Potato Soup with Peas and Caraway	66
Potato Stew, Carrot and	68
Potatoes, Herrings in Cream with	72
Potatoes with Dip, Grilled	71
Potatoes with Quark, Jacket	71
Potatoes with Tsatsiki, Spiced	69
Potatoes with Brussels Sprouts, Fried	72
Quark, Jacket Potatoes with	71
Quark, Strawberry	40
Quark Bread with Carrot Slices	26
Quark Crumb Cake	34
Quark Pudding, Custard and	28
Quark Stollen	33
Radish Bread	27
Raspberry Sorbet	45
Rice with Mixed Mushrooms	84
Rice Pudding	96
Rice Salad	89
Rissoles with Vegetables	115
Salad, Alpine Vegetable Cheese	56
Salad, Beetroot	51
Salad, Carrot and Pear	56
Salad, Celeriac	57
Salad, Chicken and Lentil Sprouts	112
Salad, Fennel and Celery	56
Salad, Fennel with Fruit	54
Salad, Italian	49
Salad, Mexican Bean	52
Salad, Mixed Bean Sprout	48
Salad, Mixed with Salmon	124
Salad, Mixed Vegetable	76
Salad, Plaice Fillets with Cucumber	125
Salad, Potato with Herrings	74
Salad, Raw Cauliflower	52
Salad, Rice	89
Salad, Scrambled Eggs with Warm Vegetable	108
Salad, Summer with Sprouts	48
Salad, Swiss Bean	110
Salad, Tomato and Scrambled Eggs	110
Salad, Waldeck	51
Salad, Waldorf Chicken	112
Salad, Wheat with Sheep's Cheese	96
Salmon, Mixed Salad with	124
Salmon Fillet with Mixed Vegetables	121
Sauerkraut, Corn Dumplings with	95
Sauerkraut, Mashed Potato and Fried Onion with	72
Sesame Sticks	38
Sorbet, Raspberry	45

Soufflé, Courgette	102
Soup, Asparagus	60
Soup, Country Tomato	63
Soup, Courgette and Potato	66
Soup, Cream of Celeriac	62
Soup, Fish	121
Soup, Middle European Iced Cherry	45
Soup, Millet	60
Soup, Pancake Strip	58
Soup, Paprika Cream	59
Soup, Pepper and Cabbage	63
Soup, Potato and Leek	66
Soup, Potato with Peas and Caraway	66
Soup, Vegetable	60
Soup, Vegetable with Cheese Dumplings	77
Spaghetti with Garlic Cream Sauce	79
Spaghetti with Spicy Tomato Sauce	78
Spaghetti on Vegetables	81
Spinach Gratin	71
Spinach and Minced Meat Bake	115
Strawberry Drink	40
Strawberry Quark	40
Tagliatelle with Vegetable Sauce	81
Tomato Salad and Scrambled Eggs	110
Tomato Sauce, Spaghetti with Spicy	78
Tomato Soup, Country	63
Trout, Blue	122
Tsatsiki, Spiced Potatoes with	69
Turkey Cream Steaks with Beans	110
Turkey Roll with Leek Almond Vegetables	109
Vegetable Cheese Salad, Alpine	56
Vegetable and Mushroom Fry	84
Vegetable Omelette	107
Vegetable Paella	91
Vegetable Pilau	89
Vegetable Salad, Mixed	76
Vegetable Salad, Scrambled Eggs with Warm	108
Vegetable Sauce, Tagliatelle with	81
Vegetable Soup,	60
Vegetable Soup with Cheese Dumplings	77
Vegetables, Grilled	102
Vegetables, Mixed Rice with	86
Vegetables, Raw Nuts with	51
Vegetables, Rissoles with	115
Vegetables, Salmon Fillet with Mixed	121
Vegetables, Spaghetti on	81
Vitamin C Bombe	42
Yoghurt, Pineapple	40

foulsham
Yeovil Road, Slough, Berkshire SL1 4JH

ISBN 0-572-01942-4

The English Language Edition

Copyright © 1993 W. Foulsham & Co. Ltd;
Originally published by © Falken-Verlag GmbH, Niedernhausen, TS, Germany.
All rights to photographs reserved by Falken-Verlag.

Phototypeset in Great Britain by: Typesetting Solutions, Slough, Berks.
Printed in Slovakia